BLUE NOTE
VOLUME 2

EDITED BY GRAHAM MARSH AND GLYN CALLINGHAM

COLLINS & BROWN

First published in Great Britain in 1997
by Collins & Brown Limited
The Chrysalis Building
Bramley Road
London W10 6SP

An imprint of Chrysalis Books Group plc

Copyright © Graham Marsh and Glyn Callingham 1997

The right of Graham Marsh and Glyn Callingham to be identified
as the authors of this work has been asserted by them in
accordance with the Copyright, Designs and Patents Act, 1998.

3 5 7 9 8 6 4 2

British Library Cataloguing-in-Publication Data:
A catalogue record for this book is available from
the British Library.

ISBN 1 85585 416 3

Record sleeves are reproduced by kind permission of
EMI, London and Blue Note/Capitol Records, New York.

Art Direction and Design by Graham Marsh

DTP assistance: Simon Ward-Hastelow

Printed and bound in China by SNP Leefung

For June, with love. GM

For Kate, Ruth and Hannah, three true originals. GC

ACKNOWLEDGEMENTS

SPECIAL THANKS TO:
Richard Busiakiewicz for his generous cover loan,
likewise Jack Docherty and Mike Doyle. And Ruth Lion
and Wayne Adams for their invaluable help.

ALSO THE FOLLOWING MUST GET THEIRS . . .
Mike Gavin
All at Ray's Jazz, 180 Shaftesbury Avenue, London
Geoff Dann/Sleeve Photography
EMI, London
Blue Note Records, New York
Bruce Lundvall
Michael Cuscuna
Charlie Lourie
Tony Harlow
Wendy Furness
Felix Cromey
Justin Morgan at G.H. Bass
The Crew from the Island
Max and Coco Katz
Brooks Brothers
Kate MacPhee
Julia Ward-Hastelow
Ian Shipley
Dean Rudland

© Ruth Lion

Blue Note chiefs Alfred Lion and Francis Wolff in the mid-50s.

CONTENTS

AUTHOR'S NOTE

This is not intended as a discography, just some more essential Blue Note sleeves. All illustrations are taken from actual covers, most being original issues, which accounts for why some are not pristine.

FOREWORD BY RUTH LION
BLUE NOTE – 'THE LUCKY LABEL'

In his later years, Alfred Lion was fond of referring to Blue Note as 'the lucky label'. Indeed it was for many of the artists who made their early records for the label, among whom were Thelonious Monk, Bud Powell, Lou Donaldson, Art Blakey, Horace Silver, Jackie McLean, Herbie Hancock, Freddie Hubard, Jimmy Smith and many others.

Through the years, Blue Note became known among fledgling jazz artists as *the* company to record for in order to get a head start on a promising career. This was partly because of Alfred and his partner Frank Wolff's astute overall knowledge of jazz combined with their warm personal appreciation of the artists themselves. This combination helped create a musical rapport from which emerged a tremendous creative energy.

It resulted, over the years, in the jazz catalogue for which the label is now famous. As Dexter Gordon observed to me following a rehearsal in 1956, 'You just have to play better for Blue Note.' The label was also 'lucky' for other artists, among them Gil Melle, who made his first records for Blue Note in the early 50s. Today Gil is one of Hollywood's most successful music composers for movies and television.

Later in the 50s, Blue Note became one of the first clients of designer Reid Miles. Reid created hundreds of covers which became a virtual trademark. His career continued its upward spiral when he became one of Hollywood's most prominent producers of television commercials.

At about the same time in the 50s, Rudy Van Gelder was just getting started when his friend Gil Melle took Alfred over to his studio in Hakensack, New Jersey. The rest is recording history. Rudy developed the distinctive 'Blue Note Sound' and, at the same time, became one of the most sought after engineers in jazz.

Finally, the person for whom Blue Note was the luckiest was Alfred Lion himself. He said that he was never happier than when in the midst of a recording session that was going well. These recording sessions were the very life's blood of the Blue Note experience. They were vibrant, exciting and so filled with soul soothing sounds. One session in particular stands out in my memory. It was the first time I heard the Three Sounds record at Rudy Van Gelder's studio.

The beat, the drive and the just out of this world sounds Gene Harris and his trio played that night, turned me on so that I couldn't stop dancing. The 'Twist' was a new dance sensation of the 60s, and I guess anybody there who didn't

Ruth Mason, later Ruth Lion, was the Cover Model for this 1960 Blue Note Album. See page 87.

know how to do it learned with me, twisting all over the studio, all night, with only a break between takes and then off again as soon as the guys started up.

The next most memorable sessions for me were the ones that became the magnificent Donald Byrd album *I'm Trying To Get Home*. It was certainly Alfred and Frank's most ambitious endeavour and the results more than justified the tense, nervous weeks of preparation that preceded the sessions.

Blue Note had never had such a gigantic 'all star' event to prepare for. First, there were Donald, Stanley Turrentine, Herbie Hancock, Freddie Roach, Grant Green and Bob Cranshaw. Then, on trumpets, there were heavy hitters Ernie Royal, Snooky Young, Jimmy Owens and Clark Terry. Poor Alfred was so upset with rehearsals, arrangements and with eight singers to be carrying the lead, it was almost more than he and Frank could handle. Duke Pearson was a big help, as was Coleridge Perkinson, who directed the musicians and singers. When I listen to it today, 30 years later, I only experience the spiritual essence of those great artists working together to create a musical masterpiece.

I feel sure that being in the midst of all that wonderful music helped keep Alfred and Frank going all those years. However, in the early 60s their health began to show the strain of keeping Blue Note afloat. By 1967 Alfred retired and shortly after, Frank passed away.

After years of quiet retirement in Mexico, Alfred and I returned to the States and began a more musically active life in Rancho Bernardo, a suburb of San Diego. We were able to keep in closer touch with our friends Reid Miles, Gil Melle and Leonard Feather. At this time Alfred met Michael Cuscuna and Charlie Lourie whose firm, Mosaic Records, was reissuing some of the then unavailable Blue Note recordings.

Though in exceedingly frail health, Alfred was none the less exuberant over the young men's enthusiastic interest in the Blue Note artists he remembered so well. When they spoke of saxophonists Tina Brooks and Ike Quebec, it took him back to the old days with a great sense of appreciation for the life he'd been able to live in the midst of all that great jazz music.

That wasn't the end of his personal pleasure. Shortly afterwards he received a telegram from Blue Note President, Bruce Lundvall, and Artist and Repertoire Director, Michael Cuscuna, to be a guest of honour at the 'One Night With Blue Note' concert.

Attending the concert at New York's Town Hall in February 1985, was like old home week for Alfred. Going to rehearsals, seeing all his old musician friends 'The Cats', and hearing that wonderful live jazz, was something he had never expected to experience again.

In addition, the concert put him in the intense glare of the jazz entertainment spotlight, Blue Note's founder was back. With old friends and jazz aficionados now knowing where to contact him, phone calls and letters began coming in to our San Diego home from all over the world. In the last two years of his life, Alfred was in renewed contact with old friends Miles Davis and all time favourite from the early days, Dexter Gordon, whose performance in the motion picture *Round Midnight*, touched him deeply.

As if all those happenings weren't a terrific plenty for Alfred, he was then invited to be a guest of honour at the Blue Note Jazz Festival at Mount Fuji in Japan. The music was out of this world and when Alfred gave a speech he was given a standing ovation by 30,000 fans. Looking back it appears to me that at the end of the festival, Alfred's life in jazz came practically full circle.

It's really sort of strange, but the last thing that happened before we left Tokyo was a nostalgic meeting with Hitoshi Namekata of Toshiba EMI Limited, Yasuki Nakayama, editor of the *Swing Journal*, Yoshitsuga Hirose of Nippon Television and producer of the Blue Note Mount Fuji Jazz Festival, and Dr

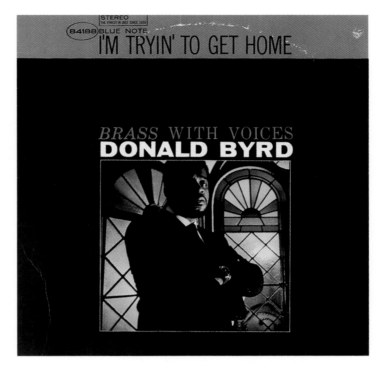

Title I'M TRYIN TO GET HOME 4188   Artist DONALD BYRD   Date 1964
Photo and Design REID MILES

Takao Ogawa, author of the *Swing Journal* column, 'I love Jazz,' who had volunteered his medical services during Alfred's visit as his personal physician.

We had lunch together and then Mr Nakayama and his friends presented Alfred with a compact disc copy of the Carnegie Hall concert 'From Spirituals to Swing'. The 1938/39 concert featured, among others, the Count Basie Original Orchestra, the Benny Goodman Sextet, Albert Ammons, Meade Lux Lewis, Lester Young, Buck Clayton and Sidney Bechet.

Alfred had gone to the concert and was flabbergasted by the exuberant boogie woogie pianists Albert Ammons and Mead Lux Lewis. Almost before he knew it, he had decided he had to try and capture that exciting sound and pulsating vibrant beat on record. The result of the subsequent success of the Ammons/Lewis recording was that Alfred had founded Blue Note and was on the way to nearly 30 years of producing the kind of jazz records for which Blue Note became famous.

Looking ahead to the 21st century and Blue Note, it is gratifying to know that, under the astute musical leadership of Bruce Lundvall and Michael Cuscuna, there are an exciting roster of brilliant young musicians ready to take their places on the world jazz scene.

RUTH LION
Ruth was with Alfred Lion for over 30 years.

Reid Miles in his Hollywood Studio with his 1946 MGTC and 1933 Lincoln.

John Hermansader, Alfred Lion, Reid Miles. Below: Reid Miles in the late 50s.

Reid Miles with Alfred and Ruth Lion.

6

MILES AHEAD

Reid Miles was born in Chicago on the 4th of July 1927, American Independence Day, a very appropriate date for someone who made his reputation – the second time around – photographing what is referred to as Americana. A kind of Norman Rockwell with a camera. His father, a candy maker, is credited with inventing the jelly bean and candy orange slice. When the stock market crashed in 1929, Miles' parents split up and he and his mother moved to Long Beach, California, where he was raised in the shadows of the shipyards and fish canneries.

After High School, Miles did a hitch in the Navy, during the final months of World War II. 'I'd like to think they ended the war because I joined up,' he said. Though he had a soft job as a chauffeur to a Captain, he despised it after a short time. The feeling was mutual: Miles was caught stealing tyres and sent to Alaska. After his (amazingly enough, honourable) discharge, he headed back to Los Angeles.

Reid Miles might have become a gas station attendant, 'I was ready to buy a gas station and pump gas.' Instead, he enrolled at Chouinard Art Institute – not because of any lofty ambitions – 'I went to art school because of a girl I was going with and because of the GI bill and it was nice to be close to her and go to an easy art school. The girl didn't work out – but three months later, it just clicked.' He had found what he wanted out of his life.

A short time later, in the early 50s, he headed for New York to look for a job with the biggest portfolio he could find. 'If it didn't fit on the desk, I wasn't talking to the right person. You need a fierce competition to do good work and when I started out, I would be competing against 11 other people for a job as an assistant to an art director at a little agency with starting pay at $48 a week. I was living at the 'Y' [MCA] for $2 a day and it was FABULOUS.'

John Hermansader gave Miles his first job in New York, and his first overcoat. Reid had just come from sunny California and certainly wasn't prepared for a New York winter. Miles was learning a tiny bit about design and how to spec type. One of Hermansader's clients was Blue Note Records, which eventually led to Reid's involvement. Alfred Lion and Francis Wolff were so taken by Miles' innovative designs, he went on to design almost 500 Blue Note record sleeves during a period of some 15 years in the late 50s, early 60s.

A year and a half later Miles landed a job with *Esquire* magazine, taking with him the Blue Note account and the assurance from the magazine, and all subsequent employers, that he could continue his work for the label. Hired to do paste-up, Miles was soon elevated to status of art director. But the job didn't last long, ending primarily because of Miles' acknowledged inability to see two sides of an issue. 'I've always been very definitive. I see things in black and white terms,' Miles admitted. 'As far as I'm concerned, there are no shades of grey.'

The job at *Esquire* was only the first that ended because of arguments over creative control. For nine years, Miles worked for more agencies and magazines than he could remember. 'They would hire you for the strength of your portfolio, and then ask you to do crap! At one point in New York, I'd been in and out of so many agencies that Andy Warhol pleaded with Margaret Hockaday to give me a job. I was at her agency for a couple of years, when I slipped off in a client meeting. I'm no politician. The next day Margaret, the perfect, controlled lady, gave me the word, "Reid, may be you belong in your own business." New York taught me to scream. That's its claim to fame.'

Finally, with the encouragement of photographers Art Kane and Melvin Sokolsky, he left his job at Columbia Records to become a photographer. At first, like most of the other photographers of the late 60s, it was 35mm wide angle and super divine. By 1971 he was making 25 trips a year between coasts, which led to his permanent return to Los Angeles. Here he discovered the wonderful character actors and actresses of movies and television. They, along with remembering the experiences of his own childhood and the wonderful down-the-middle-of-the-road charm of the *Saturday Evening Post* covers, influenced the images that brought Miles the most recognition as a photographer.

His clients have included *Saturday Evening Post*, *Look*, *Esquire*, most major automotive corporations, Kawasaki, Honda, Kelloggs, Raleigh and Virginia Slims cigarettes, Dole, DuPont, Polaroid, celebrities, and countless others. Television commercial production accounted for as much as 25% of the annual billings.

'You can't just photograph garbage without restyling it. I think any designer, illustrator or first-rate photographer knows this. That's a matter of design, control, playing one shape against another. That's basic. But how many guys know that? Ten guys in the country realise how important that is.'

Reid Miles continued working in his Hollywood studio until his death in early 1993.

WAYNE ADAMS
(Wayne Adams/Reid Miles Studio, Hollywood, CA.)

Dippin' in the bag! Flyers and DJ's calling cards the Blue Note way.

HOME COOKIN'

It's the mid-80s and the Blue Note label is being relaunched. Jazz, in those dark, far off days, was to most people about murky pubs and Kenny Baker. Any thoughts of cool modernist lines were strictly the preserve of a handful of media types who seemed to be determined to recreate *Absolute Beginners* from inside whichever Soho watering hole they preferred that week. Worse than this, with little obvious demand it was very difficult to get hold of any records that would compliment your Dean Swift phase. Once you had run through the obvious Miles and Trane, and a handful of Hammond classics that had sold well on initial release, the racks were a sorry sight. This was about to change.

Blue Note's relaunch meant that a handful of classic albums could be found in every suburban record store, standing out like a pair of Weejuns in their immaculate Reid Miles tailoring. If you were trying to find the way in, who could fail with a copy of Herbie Hancock's *Taking Off* (my first Blue Note), so cool in white and black. Through this logic my second Blue Note had to be Eric Dolphy's oddly beclocked *Out to Lunch*, which in my jazz naivety, I didn't even notice was inaccessible. Jazz was back, and as a whole world-wide club scene started to develop, Blue Note was always going to be first off the block.

EMI's reissue programme could only ever touch the surface of a label that had released over 700 albums in its ever moving past. Gilles Peterson was drafted in, and the stunning Blue Series appeared, whetting appetites for the seriously obscure. Suddenly you knew that Patton's *Latona* and Don Wilkerson's *Dem Tambourines* sounded as good as you'd always suspected. But this was nothing to the man who had witnessed an original Blue Note inner sleeve from the 60s, with its depiction of obscure, and no doubt brilliant, albums of ultimate rarity.

But jazz clubbing was seeing a change as the 4/4 beat of House invaded mainstream clubland with a vengeance in 1988. This sleazy export from Chicago obliterated all-comers, sending Hip Hop back underground and consigning the previously dominant rare groove funk scene to an early grave. Jazz, however, with a sharp twist that saw its prime movers name it Acid Jazz (a tongue-in-cheek reference to Acid House), became the only clubland alternative to House, first in the UK and then around the globe. As preferences switched from Hard Bop to the Hammond Boogaloo, everyone always wanted a Blue Note. First Lou Donaldson, then 'Groove' Holmes and as record dealers who had previously specialized in soul started trawling the States for jazz albums, anyone willing to part with the requisite cash could develop a Blue Note collection.

So, from a joke designed to get some extra work for a few DJs, the whole Acid Jazz thing developed a life of its own. Maybe it was the emphasis on good live acts, perhaps the wide range of music from 50s Afro-Cuban jazz to the latest Hip Hop played in the clubs. It was a scene that had its own culture; clothes, record labels and clubs, and although it was resolutely dedicated to new music (it was the place that many of today's most talked-about labels – stand up Mo Wax, Dorado – kicked off), its whole style paid more than passing respect to the classic Blue Note style of Reid Miles' sleeves and Francis Wolff's photography.

This found focus in 1991 when Blue Note in the UK reactivated the Blue Series and the first volume of this book was published. Suddenly you could have the DJs favourite records without upsetting the bank manager. While in every record shop in the land your eyes would be greeted with new records whose sleeves paid homage at the altar of Reid Miles. It could be the blindingly obvious: The Young Disciples *Apparently Nothing*, a take on Joe Henderson's *Mode For Joe*. A little more subtle was the same group's debut album which gave a nod to Herbie Hancock's *Inventions and Dimensions*. The counter would groan under the weight of flyers 'inspired' by the boys at W61st St. It was possible to discuss the cover of your latest release with the designer (as I did) using *The Cover Art of Blue Note Records* as a reference point.

Clubs sprang up first in Europe then in Japan, and before long they appeared in the States and Australia, all getting off on one of the strangest mixtures of music ever to rock a floor. Bands such as the Brand New Heavies and Jamiroquai became international hits and it all seemed a long way from the Wag Club.

And now? As with all scenes its advances and mutations have changed it out of all recognition and the clubs that play the classic 'Notes' have disappeared back underground. In the mainstream its shock waves are everywhere; be it Reid Miles-style typography on TV adverts, or the most talked about record labels, many of whom sprung out of the Acid Jazz thing. It may seem a long way from Blakey to Drum and Bass, but in many ways its just the same old British thing; an undying love of the best black music. Its just a thought to hold, but remember that Lee Morgan's *Sidewinder* is now on to its third, or possibly fourth, generation of UK clubbers.

DEAN RUDLAND

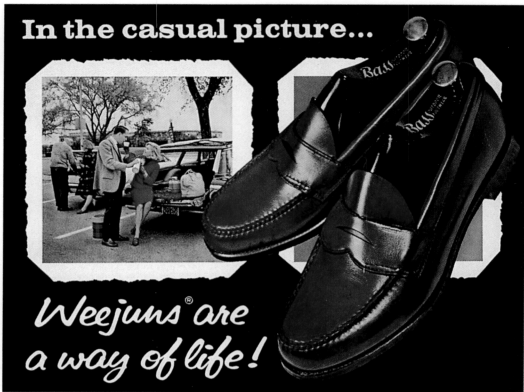

COOL STRUTTIN'

If there is no immediate association between the name George Bass and those celebrated icons of celluloid and vinyl, there should be. At some time or another, from Robert Mitchum to Thelonious Monk, all have worn the Weejun Penny Loafer, courtesy of Mr Bass. His loafers were, and still are, one of the rare and enduring items of standard-issue cool.

Once an indispensable part of the 'preppie' look, Bass Weejuns with their clean, smooth lines, soon became the unapproachably correct shoe of New York's hipster saints during those fabled pre-psychedelic 60s. They complimented perfectly the sleek, sharp and minimal look that the modernists had nailed down so completely. If Miles Davis had the green shirt and Jimmy Smith the sweaters, the rest of the congregation for sure had the Weejuns.

The loafer was introduced to Americans in 1936 by George Bass, who at the time was taking care of business at G.H. Bass & Co. Legend has it that Mr B adapted his new shoe from the traditional Norwegian fisherman's slipper, calling it Weejun in acknowledgement of its Norse origins. Ironically, the Norwegian shoe itself was based on the American Indian moccasin.

The Weejun soon became a symbol of American casual style. These loafers were so comfortable and hip you could put them on with your hands in your pockets, a sometimes overlooked fact, but worthy of special mention in dispatches. The Penny Loafer tag came about after a craze started by women who slipped pennies into the 'saddle' at the front of their loafers.

When the powers that be instigate a museum of cult objects, a pair of Weejuns will undoubtedly be displayed alongside a pair of Levi 501 XX 1955 model blue jeans, an all cotton Burberry Trenchcoat and a Brooks Brothers button-down shirt. Indeed it is a considered opinion, at least by some people of my acquaintance – to whom these things matter – that apart from the two great art forms of Jazz and Film that the USA has surfaced this century, the third might just be the Weejun.

Although endlessly copied by a host of imitators, the casual shoe by which all others are judged, is still the original Bass Weejun moccasin-style loafer, with its hand-sewn front, leather soles and heels, worn with or without socks. It looks better, and becomes more comfortable after each wearing, as it takes on the shape of your foot. As George Frazier, the late, great tastemaster and doyen of Boston journalists, said: 'Wanna know if a guy's well dressed? Look down.'

GRAHAM MARSH

COVER STORY

The benefits to jazz from Columbia's successful introduction of the long play record in 1948, were immense. No longer restricted to the three minute per side of the 78 era, jazz could now be recorded in real time and the rapid expansion of record labels issuing jazz only, was immediate.

By the mid-50s the 12-inch version, with a total needle time of 50 minutes, had become the standard format, its microgrooves replaying all the major and minor moves in jazz for the next three decades, until the advent of the compact disc.

If the LP carried the jazz message to a wider audience, then the protective sleeve it was sold in offered similar potential for innovation. The 50s jazz graphics led the field in sleeve design.

Late 1955 saw Blue Note enter this market with their first 12-inch issues. The following year Reid Miles, a young commercial artist working in the art department at *Esquire* magazine, became the label's main designer. An avid classical music fan, he relied on Blue Note chief Alfred Lion to describe the mood and intent of each album. He then created an endless array of pin-sharp graphic designs, often combined with Francis Wolff's photographs, that over the next 11 years transcended mere commercial considerations, gave the distinctive Blue Note look and became an art form in its own right.

As Wolff once said, 'We established a style including recording, pressing and covers. The details made the difference.'

GLYN CALLINGHAM

Title THE JAZZ MESSENGERS AT THE CAFE BOHEMIA Vol. 1 1507
Artist THE JAZZ MESSENGERS
Date 1955
Photo FRANCIS WOLFF
Design JOHN HERMANSADER

Title THE JAZZ MESSENGERS AT THE CAFE BOHEMIA Vol. 2 1508
Artist THE JAZZ MESSENGERS
Date 1955
Photo FRANCIS WOLFF
Design JOHN HERMANSADER

Opposite: Title THE JAZZ MESSENGERS AT THE CAFE BOHEMIA Vol. 3 BNJ 61007 Artist THE JAZZ MESSENGERS
Date RELEASED JAPAN ONLY 1984 Photo FRANCIS WOLFF Original Design JOHN HERMANSADER

THE JAZZ MESSENGERS

The Jazz Messengers AT THE CAFE BOHEMIA VOLUME 3 BLUE NOTE 61007

ORACE SILVER   HANK MOBLEY   ART BLAKEY   KENNY DORHAM   DOUG WATKINS

N·6·21

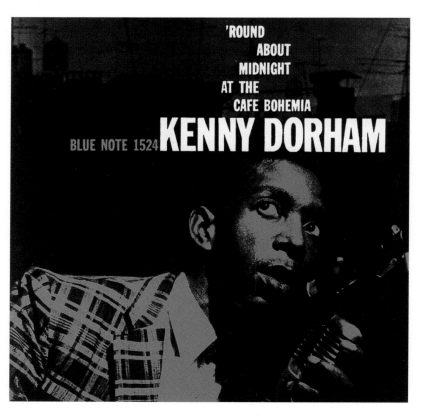

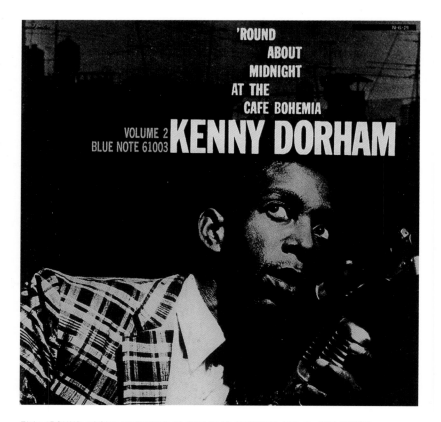

Title 'ROUND ABOUT MIDNIGHT AT THE CAFE BOHEMIA 1524
Artist KENNY DORHAM
Date 1956
Photo FRANCIS WOLFF
Design REID MILES

Title 'ROUND ABOUT MIDNIGHT AT THE CAFE BOHEMIA Vol. 2 BNJ 61003
Artist KENNY DORHAM
Date RELEASED JAPAN ONLY 1984
Photo FRANCIS WOLFF
Original Design REID MILES

Title HOLIDAY FOR SKINS Vol. 1 4004
Artist ART BLAKEY
Date 1958
Photo FRANCIS WOLFF
Design REID MILES

Title HOLIDAY FOR SKINS Vol. 2 4005
Artist ART BLAKEY
Date 1958
Photo FRANCIS WOLFF
Design REID MILES

Opposite: Title 'ROUND ABOUT MIDNIGHT AT THE CAFE BOHEMIA Vol. 3 BNJ 61004 Artist KENNY DORHAM
Date RELEASED JAPAN ONLY 1984 Photo FRANCIS WOLFF Original Design REID MILES

'ROUND
ABOUT
MIDNIGHT
AT THE
CAFE BOHEMIA

VOLUME 3
BLUE NOTE 61004 KENNY DORHAM

N·6·21

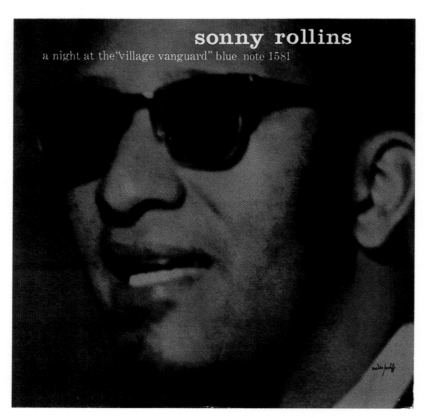

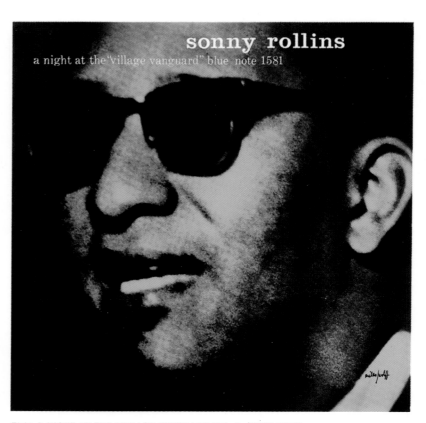

Title A NIGHT AT THE VILLAGE VANGUARD 1581
Artist SONNY ROLLINS
Date 1957
Photo FRANCIS WOLFF
Design REID MILES

Title A NIGHT AT THE VILLAGE VANGUARD Vol. 2 K18P 9277
Artist SONNY ROLLINS
Date RELEASED JAPAN ONLY 1983
Photo FRANCIS WOLFF
Original Design REID MILES

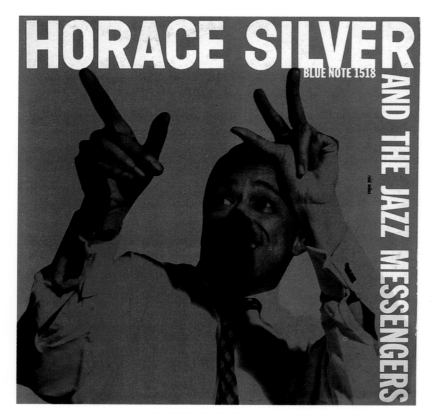

Title HORACE SILVER AND THE JAZZ MESSENGERS 1518
Artist HORACE SILVER
Date 1955
Photo FRANCIS WOLFF
Design REID MILES

Title HORACE SILVER TRIO AND ART BLAKEY-SABU 1520
Artist HORACE SILVER
Date 1955
Photo FRANCIS WOLFF
Design REID MILES

Opposite: Title A NIGHT AT THE VILLAGE VANGUARD Vol. 3 K18P 9278 Artist SONNY ROLLINS
Date RELEASED JAPAN ONLY 1983 Photo FRANCIS WOLFF Original Design REID MILES

sonny rollins

a night at the "village vanguard" blue note 1581

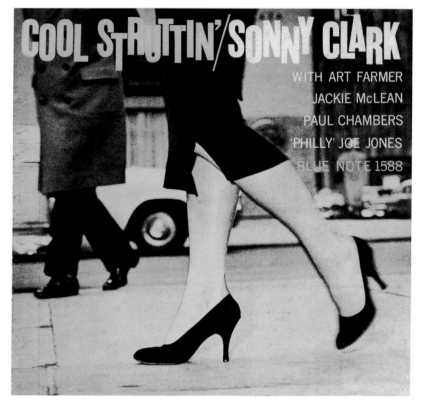

Title COOL STRUTTIN' 1588
Artist SONNY CLARK
Date 1958
Design REID MILES

"At one point in New York, I'd been in and
out of so many agencies that Andy Warhol pleaded with
Margaret Hockaday to give me a job. I was
at her agency for a couple of years, when I slipped off
in a client meeting. I'm no politician.
The next day, Margaret, the perfect, controlled, lady,
gave me the word, 'Reid, maybe you belong
in your own business'. New York taught me to scream.
That's its claim to fame."
REID MILES

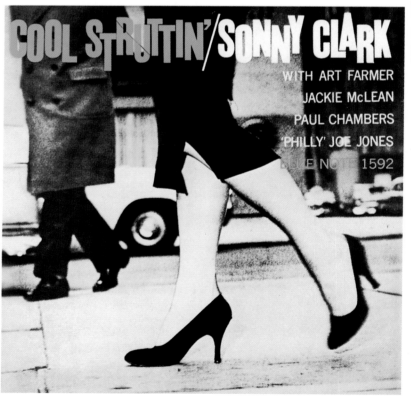

Title COOL STRUTTIN' Vol. 2 1592
Artist SONNY CLARK
Date RELEASED JAPAN ONLY 1983
Original Design REID MILES

Opposite: Title QUINTETS BNJ 61016 Artist SONNY CLARK Date RELEASED JAPAN ONLY 1985 Original Design REID MILES

SONNY CLARK QuintETS

WITH ART FARMER

JACKIE McLEAN

PAUL CHAMBERS

'PHILLY' JOE JONES

BLUE NOTE 61016

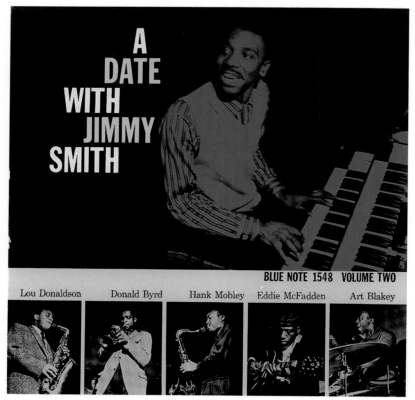

Title A DATE WITH Vol. 1 1547
Artist JIMMY SMITH
Date 1957
Photo FRANCIS WOLFF
Design REID MILES

Title A DATE WITH Vol. 2 1548
Artist JIMMY SMITH
Date 1957
Photo FRANCIS WOLFF
Design REID MILES

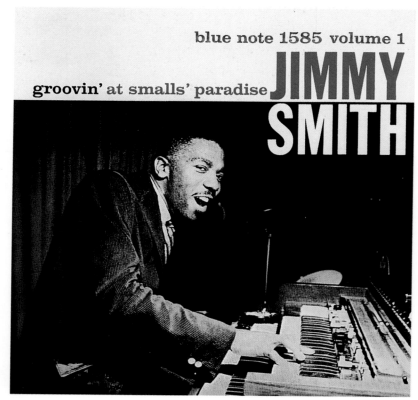

Title GROOVIN' AT SMALLS' PARADISE Vol. 1 1585
Artist JIMMY SMITH
Date 1957
Photo FRANCIS WOLFF
Design REID MILES

Title GROOVIN' AT SMALLS' PARADISE Vol. 2 1586
Artist JIMMY SMITH
Date 1957
Photo FRANCIS WOLFF
Design REID MILES

Opposite: Title BACK TO THE TRACKS 4052 Artist TINA BROOKS Date 1960 Photo FRANCIS WOLFF Design REID MILES

STEREO
THE FINEST IN JAZZ SINCE 1939
84052 BLUE NOTE

back to the tracks

TINA BROOKS
WITH BLUE MITCHELL
KENNY DREW
PAUL CHAMBERS
ART TAYLOR

6 pieces of **SILVER** HORACE SILVER quintet, blue note 1539

Title 6 PIECES OF SILVER 1539
Artist HORACE SILVER
Date 1956
Photo FRANCIS WOLFF
Design REID MILES

SENÕR BLUES HORACE SILVER rare tracks, blue note 61005

Title SENÕR BLUES BNJ 61005
Artist HORACE SILVER
Date RELEASED JAPAN ONLY 1984
Photo FRANCIS WOLFF
Original Design REID MILES

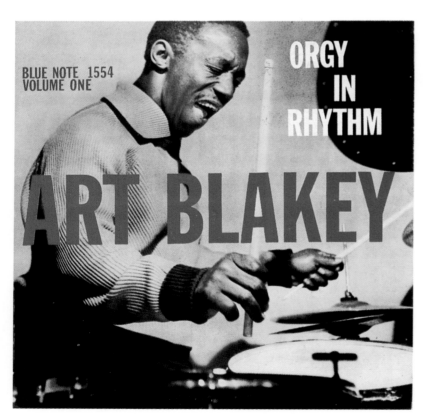

BLUE NOTE 1554 VOLUME ONE **ORGY IN RHYTHM** **ART BLAKEY**

Title ORGY IN RHYTHM Vol. 1 1554
Artist ART BLAKEY
Date 1957
Photo FRANCIS WOLFF
Design HAROLD FEINSTEIN

BLUE NOTE 1555 VOLUME TWO **ORGY IN RHYTHM** **ART BLAKEY**

Title ORGY IN RHYTHM Vol. 2 1555
Artist ART BLAKEY
Date 1957
Photo FRANCIS WOLFF
Design HAROLD FEINSTEIN

Opposite: Title CURTIS FULLER Vol. 3 1583 Artist CURTIS FULLER Date 1957 Photo FRANCIS WOLFF Design REID MILES

RT FARMER / SONNY CLARK / GEORGE TUCKER / LOUIS HAYES

CURTIS
FULLER BLUE NOTE 1583

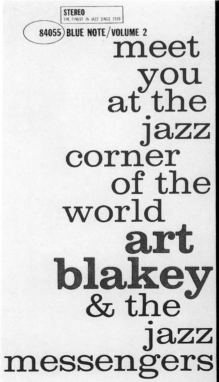

Title MEET YOU AT THE JAZZ CORNER OF THE WORLD Vol. 1 4054
Artist ART BLAKEY & THE JAZZ MESSENGERS
Date 1960
Photo HERB SNITZER
Design REID MILES

Title MEET YOU AT THE JAZZ CORNER OF THE WORLD Vol. 2 4055
Artist ART BLAKEY & THE JAZZ MESSENGERS
Date 1960
Photo HERB SNITZER
Design REID MILES

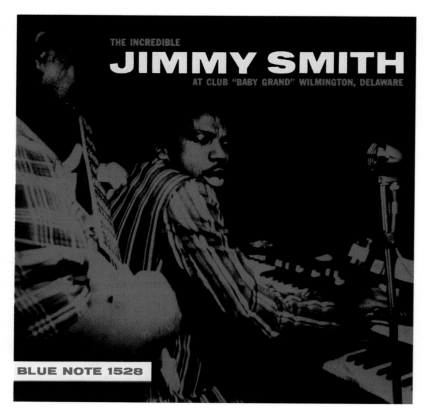
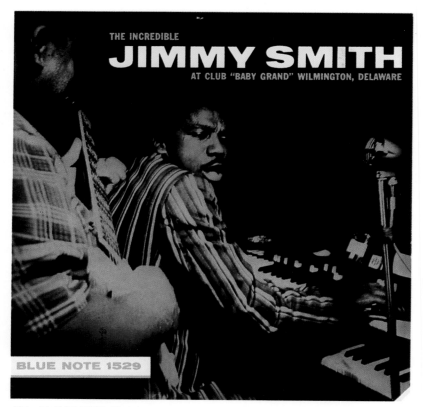

Title AT CLUB BABY GRAND Vol. 1 No 1528
Artist JIMMY SMITH
Date 1956
Photo FRANCIS WOLFF
Design REID MILES

Title AT CLUB BABY GRAND Vol. 2 1529
Artist JIMMY SMITH
Date 1956
Photo FRANCIS WOLFF
Design REID MILES

Opposite: Title SOFTLY AS A SUMMER BREEZE 4200 Artist JIMMY SMITH Date 1958 Photo JEAN-PIERRE LELOIR Design REID MILES

softly as a summer breeze

THE INCREDIBLE JIMMY SMITH

WITH KENNY BURRELL & PHILLY JOE JONES

THE FINEST IN JAZZ SINCE 1939

4200 BLUE NOTE

In the early 50s Reid Miles
headed for New York to look for a job with the
biggest portfolio he could find.
"If it didn't fit on the desk, I wasn't talking to
the right person."
REID MILES

Title A NIGHT AT BIRDLAND Vol. 1   1521
Artist ART BLAKEY
Date 1954
Photo FRANCIS WOLFF
Design REID MILES   Drawing GEORGE WRIGHT

Title A NIGHT AT BIRDLAND Vol, 3   BNJ 61002
Artist ART BLAKEY
Date RELEASED JAPAN ONLY 1984
Photo FRANCIS WOLFF
Original Design REID MILES   Drawing GEORGE WRIGHT

Opposite: Title A NIGHT AT BIRDLAND Vol. 2   1522   Artist ART BLAKEY   Date 1954   Photo FRANCIS WOLFF   Design REID MILES   Drawing GEORGE WRIGHT

A NIGHT AT BIRDLAND

ART BLAKEY

WITH
CLIFFORD BROWN
LOU DONALDSON
HORACE SILVER
CURLY RUSSELL

blue note 1522 - volume 2

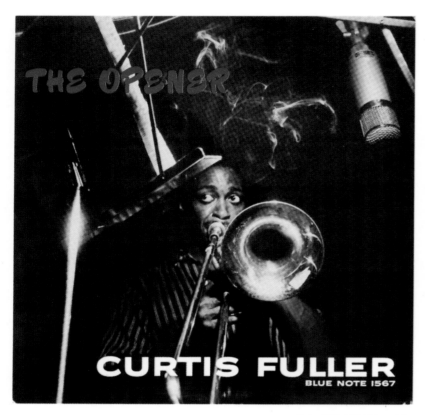

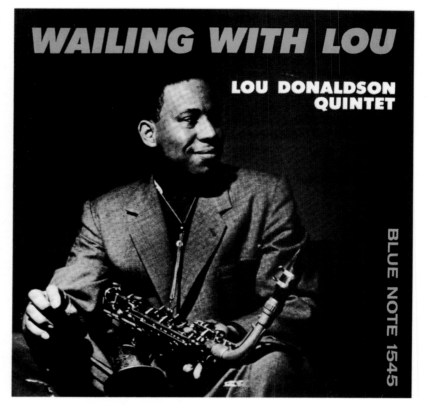

Title THE OPENER 1567
Artist CURTIS FULLER
Date 1957
Photo FRANCIS WOLFF

Title WAILING WITH LOU 1545
Artist LOU DONALDSON
Date 1955
Photo FRANCIS WOLFF
Design HAROLD FEINSTEIN

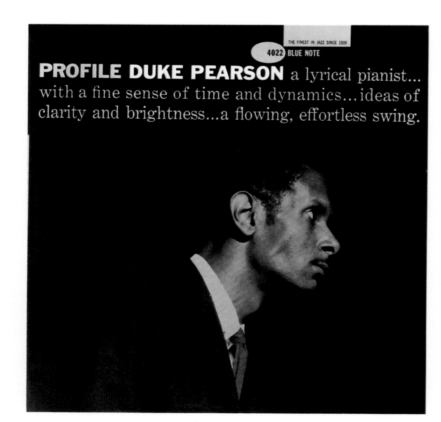

Title PROFILE 4022
Artist DUKE PEARSON
Date 1959
Photo FRANCIS WOLFF
Design REID MILES

Title INTRODUCING 1523
Artist KENNY BURRELL
Date 1956
Photo FRANCIS WOLFF
Design REID MILES

Opposite: Title WALKIN' & TALKIN' 4010 Artist BENNIE GREEN Date 1959 Photo FRANCIS WOLFF Design REID MILES

WALKIN' & TALKIN'

BENNIE GREEN BLUE NOTE 4010

Title HERE COMES LOUIS SMITH 1584
Artist LOUIS SMITH
Date 1958
Photo CHARLES LOWE

Title CLIFF CRAFT 1582
Artist CLIFFORD JORDAN
Date 1957
Photo FRANCIS WOLFF
Design REID MILES

Title SUNDAY MORNIN' 4099
Artist GRANT GREEN
Date 1961
Photo FRANCIS WOLFF
Design REID MILES

Title SOME OTHER STUFF 4177
Artist GRACHAN MONCUR III
Date 1964
Photo and Design REID MILES

Opposite: Title THE LATIN BIT 4111 Artist GRANT GREEN Date 1962 Photo and Design REID MILES

THE LATIN BIT / GRANT GREEN

Johnny Acea / Piano
Wendell Marshall / Bass
Willie Bobo / Drums
Potato Valdez / Conga
Garvin Masseaux / Chekere

STEREO
THE FINEST IN JAZZ SINCE 1939
84111 BLUE NOTE

PHOTO/DESIGN/REID MILES

Title TIME WAITS 1598
Artist BUD POWELL
Date 1958
Photo FRANCIS WOLFF
Design REID MILES

Title MOVIN' & GROOVIN' 4028
Artist HORACE PARLAN
Date 1960
Photo FRANCIS WOLFF
Design REID MILES

Title BLUE JOHN 4143
Artist JOHN PATTON
Date 1963
Photo FRANCIS WOLFF
Design REID MILES

Title TENDER FEELIN'S 4035
Artist DUKE PEARSON
Date 1959
Photo FRANCIS WOLFF
Design REID MILES

Opposite: Title SWING AND SOUL 1566 Artist LOU DONALDSON Date 1957 Photo FRANCIS WOLFF Design DAVID LUNN

swing and soul

LOU DONALDSON

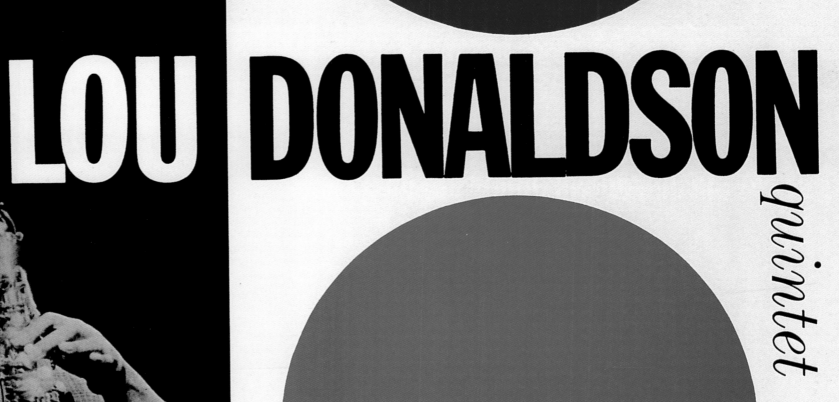

blue note 1566

quintet

design-lunn/photo-wolff

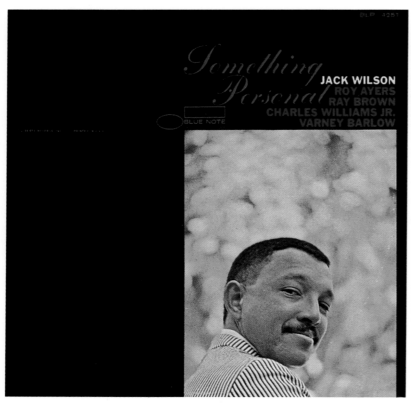

Title SOMETHING PERSONAL 4251
Artist JACK WILSON
Date 1967
Photo KEN KIM
Design REID MILES

Title THE SPOILER 4256
Artist STANLEY TURRENTINE
Date 1966
Photo FRANCIS WOLFF
Design REID MILES

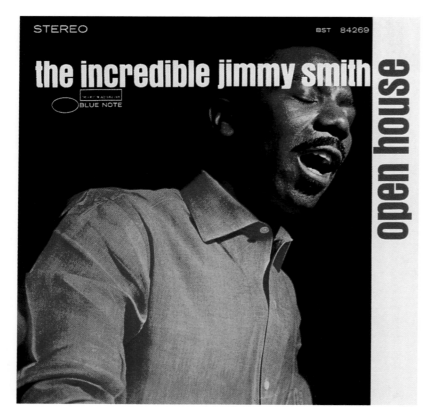

Title OPEN HOUSE 4269
Artist JIMMY SMITH
Date 1960
Photo FRANCIS WOLFF
Design REID MILES

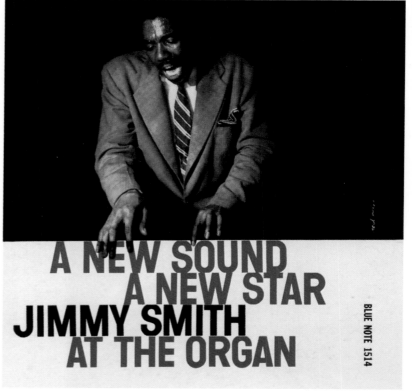

Title THE CHAMP 1514
Artist JIMMY SMITH
Date 1956
Photo FRANCIS WOLFF
Design REID MILES

Opposite: Title THE MAGNIFICENT Vol. 3 1546 Artist THAD JONES Date 1957 Photo FRANCIS WOLFF Design HAROLD FEINSTEIN

THE MAGNIFICENT THAD JONES

VOL. 3

BLUE NOTE 1546

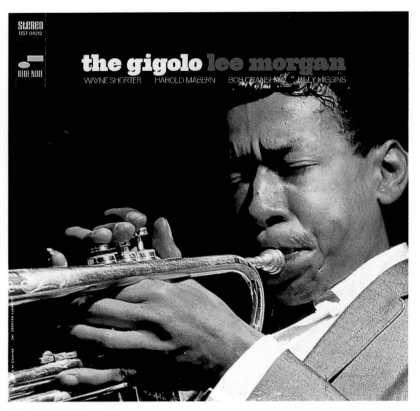

Title BUD! 1571
Artist BUD POWELL
Date 1957
Photo FRANCIS WOLFF
Design REID MILES

Title THE GIGOLO 4212
Artist LEE MORGAN
Date 1965
Photo FRANCIS WOLFF
Design FORLENZA VENOSA ASSOCIATES

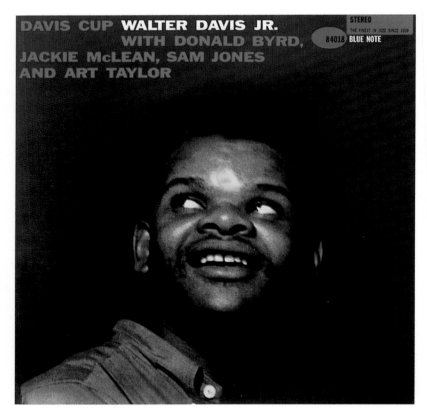

Title TENDER MOMENTS 4275
Artist MCCOY TYNER
Date 1967
Photo FRANCIS WOLFF
Design FORLENZA VENOSA ASSOCIATES

Title DAVIS CUP 4018
Artist WALTER DAVIS JR.
Date 1959
Photo FRANCIS WOLFF
Design REID MILES

Opposite: Title THE SCENE CHANGES 4009 Artist BUD POWELL Date 1958 Photo FRANCIS WOLFF Design REID MILES

the scene changes **THE AMAZING BUD POWELL**

blue note 4009

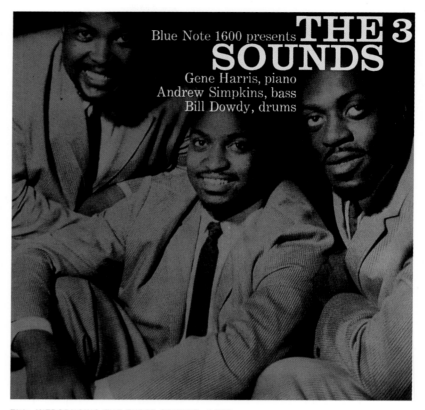

Title INTRODUCING THE THREE SOUNDS 1600
Artist THE THREE SOUNDS
Date 1958
Photo FRANCIS WOLFF
Design REID MILES

"The beat, the drive and the just out of this
world sounds Gene Harris and his trio played that night,
turned me on so that I couldn't stop dancing.
The 'Twist' was a new dance sensation of the 60s, and
I guess anybody there who didn't know how to
do it learned with me, twisting all over the studio, all
night, with only a break between takes and
then off again as soon as the guys started up."
RUTH LION

Title BLACK ORCHID 4155
Artist THE THREE SOUNDS
Date 1962
Photo FRANCIS WOLFF
Design REID MILES

Opposite: Title HEY THERE 4102 Artist THE THREE SOUNDS Date 1961 Photo FRANCIS WOLFF Design REID MILES

"Hey There,"

STEREO
THE FINEST IN JAZZ SINCE 1939
84102 BLUE NOTE

The 3 Sounds

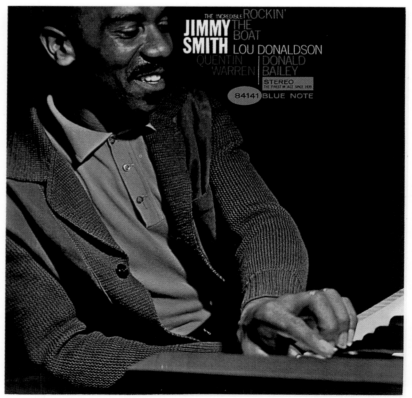

Title FURTHER EXPLORATIONS 1589
Artist HORACE SILVER
Date 1958
Photo FRANCIS WOLFF

Title BYRD IN HAND 4019
Artist DONALD BYRD
Date 1959
Photo FRANCIS WOLFF
Design REID MILES

Title LD + 3 4012
Artist LOU DONALDSON
Date 1959
Photo FRANCIS WOLFF
Design REID MILES

Title ROCKIN' THE BOAT 4141
Artist JIMMY SMITH
Date 1962
Photo FRANCIS WOLFF
Design REID MILES

Opposite: Title AT THE FIVE SPOT 4021 Artist KENNY BURRELL Date 1959 Photo FRANCIS WOLFF Design REID MILES

KENNY BURRELL
with ART BLAKEY

STEREO
THE FINEST IN JAZZ SINCE 1939

84021

BLUE NOTE

ON VIEW AT THE FIVE SPOT CAFE

Title NEW AND OLD GOSPEL 4262
Artist JACKIE MCLEAN
Date 1967
Photo FRANCIS WOLFF
Design REID MILES

Title BLUE HOUR 4057
Artist STANLEY TURRENTINE
Date 1960
Photo and Design REID MILES

Title BOTTOMS UP 4014
Artist THE THREE SOUNDS
Date 1959
Photo FRANCIS WOLFF
Design REID MILES

Title THE MUSIC FROM THE CONNECTION 4027
Artist FREDDIE REDD
Date 1960
Photo HERB SNITZER
Design REID MILES

Oppposite: Title PALO CONGO 1561 Artist SABU Date 1957 Photo FRANCIS WOLFF Design REID MILES

SABU
palo congo

BLUE NOTE 1561

Title ON THE SPUR OF THE MOMENT 4074
Artist HORACE PARLAN
Date 1961
Photo FRANCIS WOLFF
Design REID MILES

Title SOUL STIRRIN' 1599
Artist BENNIE GREEN
Date 1958
Photo FRANCIS WOLFF

Title GRANT'S FIRST STAND 4064
Artist GRANT GREEN
Date 1961
Photo FRANCIS WOLFF
Design REID MILES

Title AM I BLUE 4139
Artist GRANT GREEN
Date 1963
Photo FRANCIS WOLFF
Design REID MILES

Opposite: Title JIMMY SMITH AT THE ORGAN Vol. 1 1551 Artist JIMMY SMITH Date 1957 Photo FRANCIS WOLFF Design REID MILES

JIMMY SMITH AT THE ORGAN

with Lou Donaldson
Kenny Burrell
Art Blakey

Blue Note 1551
Volume 1

Title JUBILEE SHOUT 4122
Artist STANLEY TURRENTINE
Date 1962
Photo FRANCIS WOLFF
Design REID MILES

Title HERE 'TIS 4066
Artist LOU DONALDSON
Date 1961
Photo RONNIE BRATHWAITE
Design REID MILES

Title DEARLY BELOVED 4081
Artist STANLEY TURRENTINE
Date 1961
Photo FRANCIS WOLFF

Title LIGHT-FOOT 4053
Artist LOU DONALDSON
Date 1958
Photo FRANCIS WOLFF
Design REID MILES

Opposite: Title THE STYLINGS OF SILVER 1562 Artist HORACE SILVER Date 1957 Photo FRANCIS WOLFF

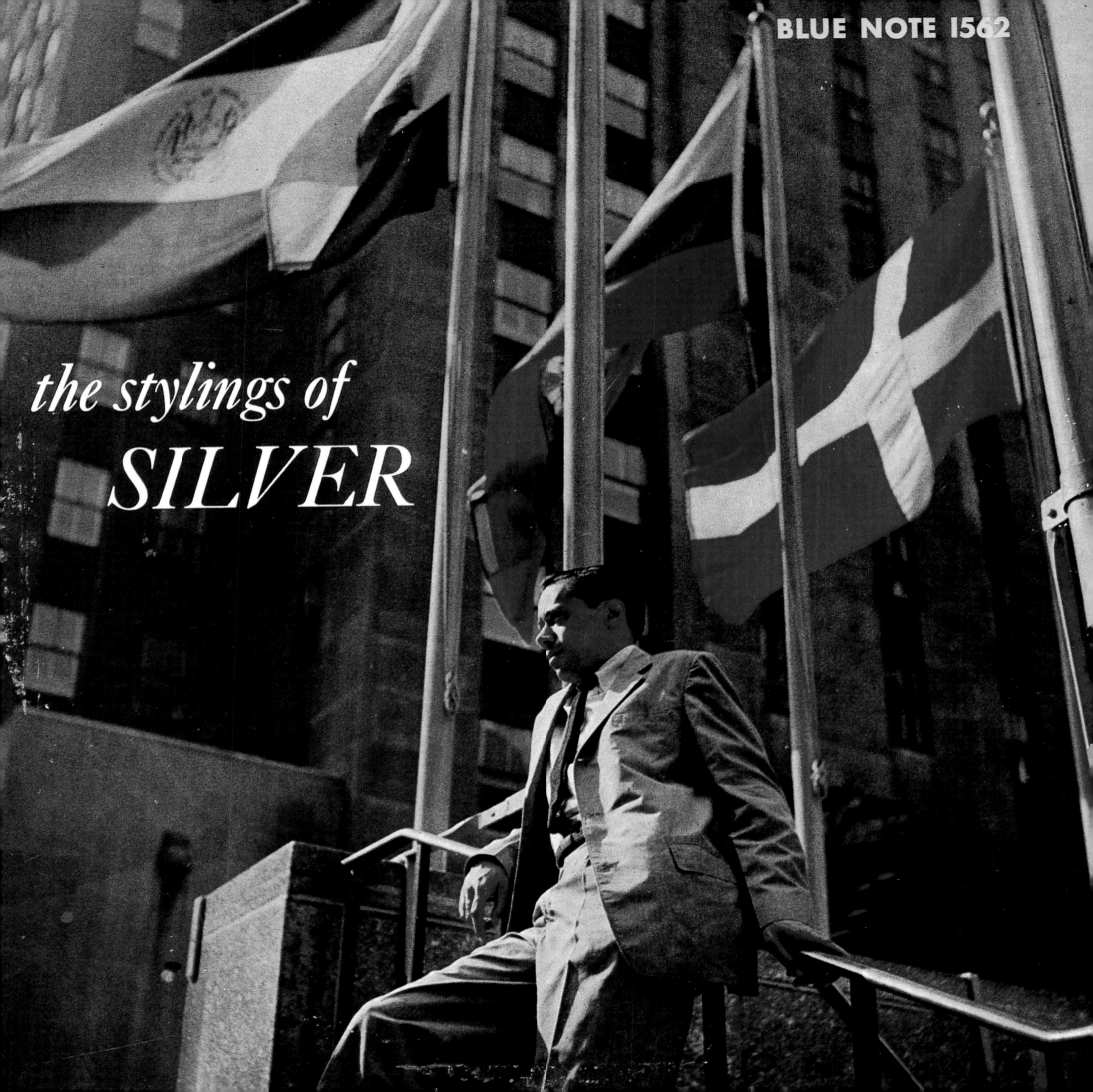

BLUE NOTE 1562

the stylings of
SILVER

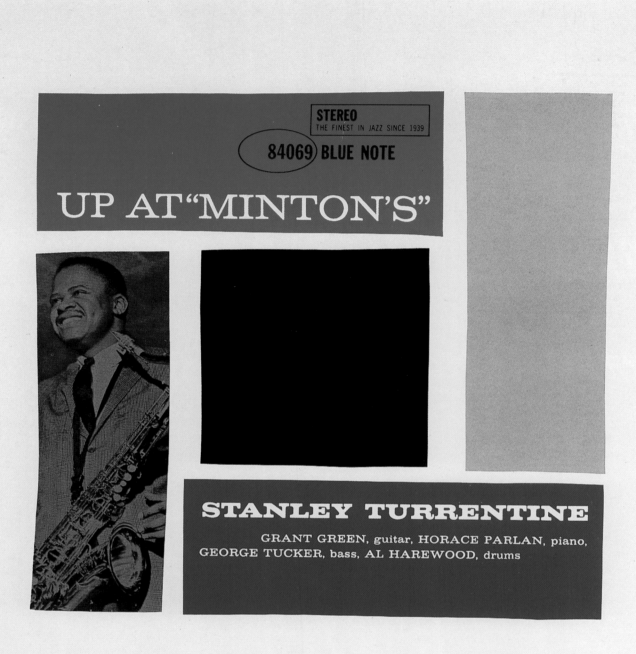

Title UP AT MINTON'S Vol. 1 4069 Artist STANLEY TURRENTINE Date 1961 Photo FRANCIS WOLFF Design REID MILES

Opposite: Title UP AT MINTON'S Vol. 2 4070 Artist STANLEY TURRENTINE Date 1961 Photo FRANCIS WOLFF Design REID MILES

STEREO
THE FINEST IN JAZZ SINCE 1939
84070 BLUE NOTE

UP AT "MINTON'S"

STANLEY TURRENTINE

GRANT GREEN, guitar, HORACE PARLAN. piano,
GEORGE TUCKER, bass, AL HAREWOOD, drums

Title EXTENSION 4171
Artist GEORGE BRAITH
Date 1965
Photo FRANCIS WOLFF
Design REID MILES

Title CONQUISTADOR 4260
Artist CECIL TAYLOR
Date 1966
Photo FRANCIS WOLFF
Design REID MILES

Title DELIGHTFULEE 4243
Artist LEE MORGAN
Date 1966
Photo FRANCIS WOLFF
Design REID MILES

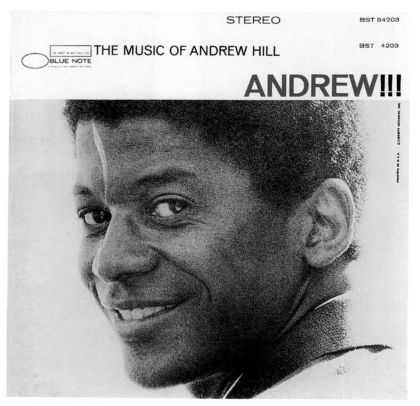

Title ANDREW 4203
Artist ANDREW HILL
Date 1964
Photo and Design REID MILES

Opposite: Title I'M MOVIN' ON 4255 Artist JIMMY SMITH Date 1963 Photo and Design REID MILES

STEREO

BST 84255

BLP 4255

THE FINEST IN JAZZ SINCE 1939
BLUE NOTE
A PRODUCT OF LIBERTY RECORDS

WITH GRANT GREEN & DONALD BAILEY

THE INCREDIBLE JIMMY SMITH

"I'M MOVIN' ON"

Title HEADS UP 4272
Artist BLUE MITCHELL
Date 1967
Photo CHARLES KEDDIE
Design FORLENZA VENOSA ASSOCIATES

Title TOTAL ECLIPSE 4291
Artist BOBBY HUTCHERSON
Date 1967
Photo FRED SELIGO
Design FORLENZA VENOSA ASSOCIATES

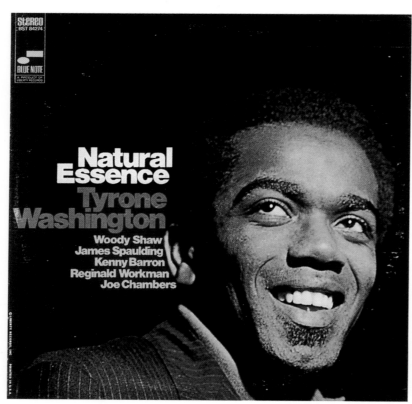

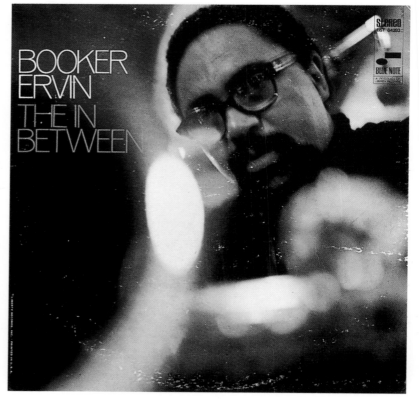

Title NATURAL ESSENCE 4274
Artist TYRONE WASHINGTON
Date 1967
Photo FRANCIS WOLFF
Design FORLENZA VENOSA ASSOCIATES

Title THE IN BETWEEN 4283
Artist BOOKER ERVIN
Date 1968
Photo FRANCIS WOLFF
Design FORLENZA VENOSA ASSOCIATES

Opposite: Title THE ALL SEEING EYE 4219 Artist WAYNE SHORTER Date 1965 Photo FRANCIS WOLFF Design REID MILES

THE ALL SEEING EYE

WAYNE SHORTER

4219 BLUE NOTE

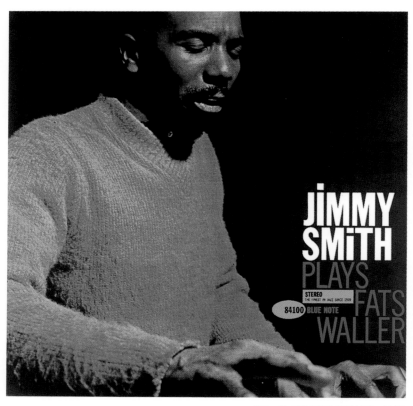

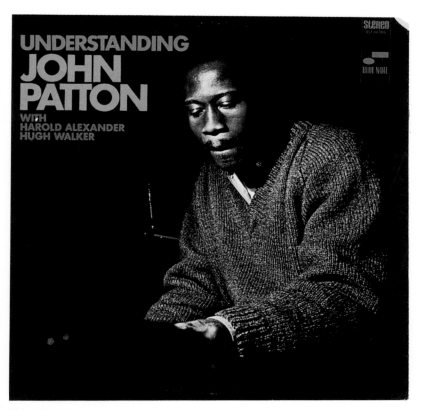

Title PLAYS FATS WALLER 4100
Artist JIMMY SMITH
Date 1962
Photo FRANCIS WOLFF
Design REID MILES

Title UNDERSTANDING 4306
Artist JOHN PATTON
Date 1968
Photo FRANCIS WOLFF

Title GREEN STREET 4071
Artist GRANT GREEN
Date 1961
Photo FRANCIS WOLFF
Design REID MILES

Title THE RIGHT TOUCH 4267
Artist DUKE PEARSON
Date 1967
Photo FRANCIS WOLFF
Design REID MILES

Opposite: Title COMIN' YOUR WAY 4065 Artist STANLEY TURRENTINE Date 1961 Photo FRANCIS WOLFF Design REID MILES

Title AT THE JAZZ CORNER OF THE WORLD Vol. 2 4016
Artist ART BLAKEY & THE JAZZ MESSENGERS
Date 1959
Photo FRANCIS WOLFF
Design REID MILES

"John Hermansader gave Reid Miles his
first job in New York, and his first overcoat. Reid had
just come from sunny California and
certainly wasn't prepared for a New York winter."
WAYNE ADAMS

Title AT THE JAZZ CORNER OF THE WORLD Vol. 1 4015
Artist ART BLAKEY & THE JAZZ MESSENGERS
Date 1959
Photo FRANCIS WOLFF
Design REID MILES

Opposite: Title CITY LIGHTS 1575 Artist LEE MORGAN Date 1957 Photo FRANCIS WOLFF Design REID MILES

CITY LIGHTS LEE MORGAN BLUE NOTE 1575

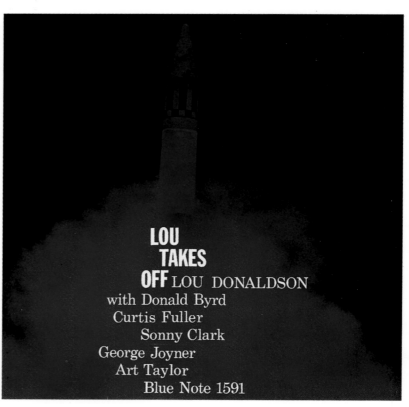

Title EMPYREAN ISLES 4175
Artist HERBIE HANCOCK
Date 1964
Photo FRANCIS WOLFF
Design REID MILES

Title LOU TAKES OFF 1591
Artist LOU DONALDSON
Date 1957

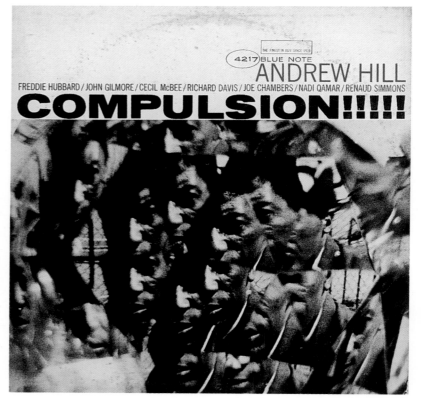

Title A BLOWING SESSION Vol. 2 1559
Artist JOHNNY GRIFFIN
Date 1957
Photo FRANCIS WOLFF
Design HAROLD FEINSTEIN

Title COMPULSION 4217
Artist ANDREW HILL
Date 1965
Photo and Design REID MILES

Opposite: Title BASS ON TOP 1569 Artist PAUL CHAMBERS Date 1957 Photo FRANCIS WOLFF Design HAROLD FEINSTEIN

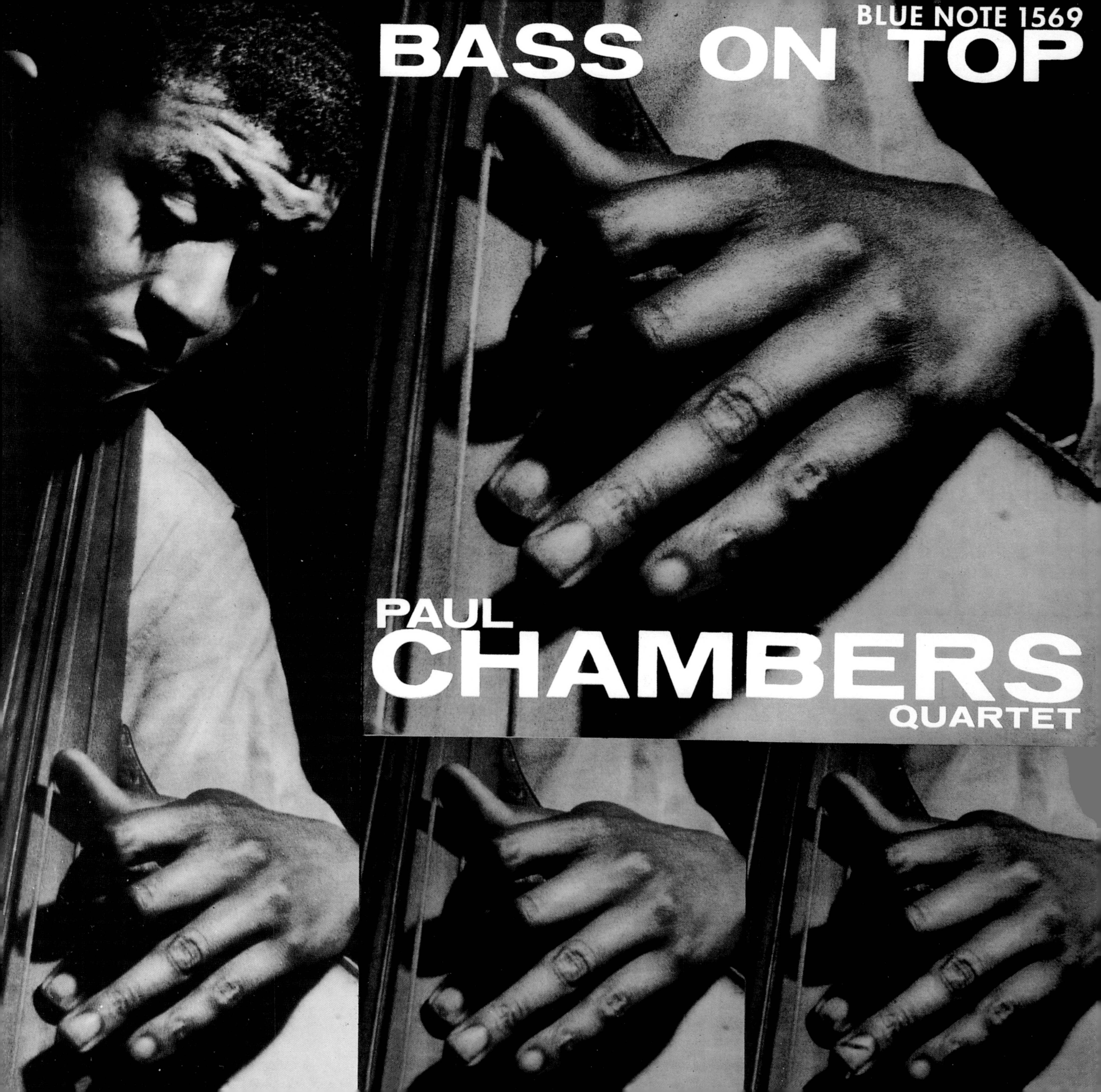

BLUE NOTE 1569

BASS ON TOP

PAUL CHAMBERS QUARTET

Title REACH OUT 4288 Artist HANK MOBLEY Date 1968 Photos BOB LAMPARD Design FORLENZA VENOSA ASSOCIATES

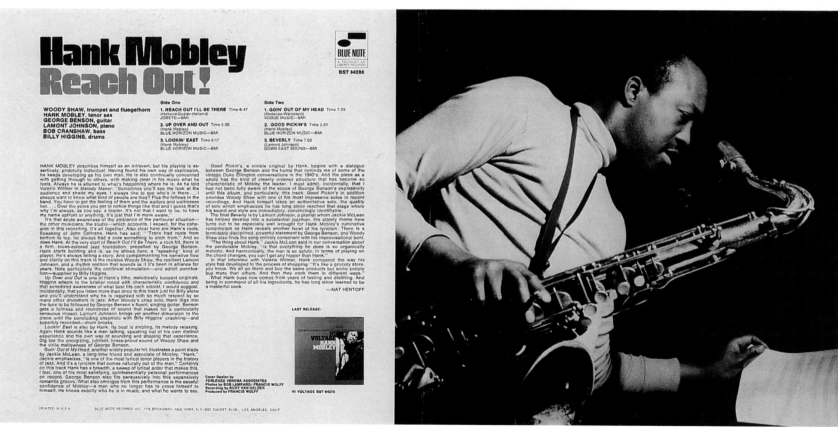

Liner Photo FRANCIS WOLFF

Opposite: Title CRAZY BABY 4030 Artist JIMMY SMITH Date 1960 Photo BOB GANLEY Design REID MILES

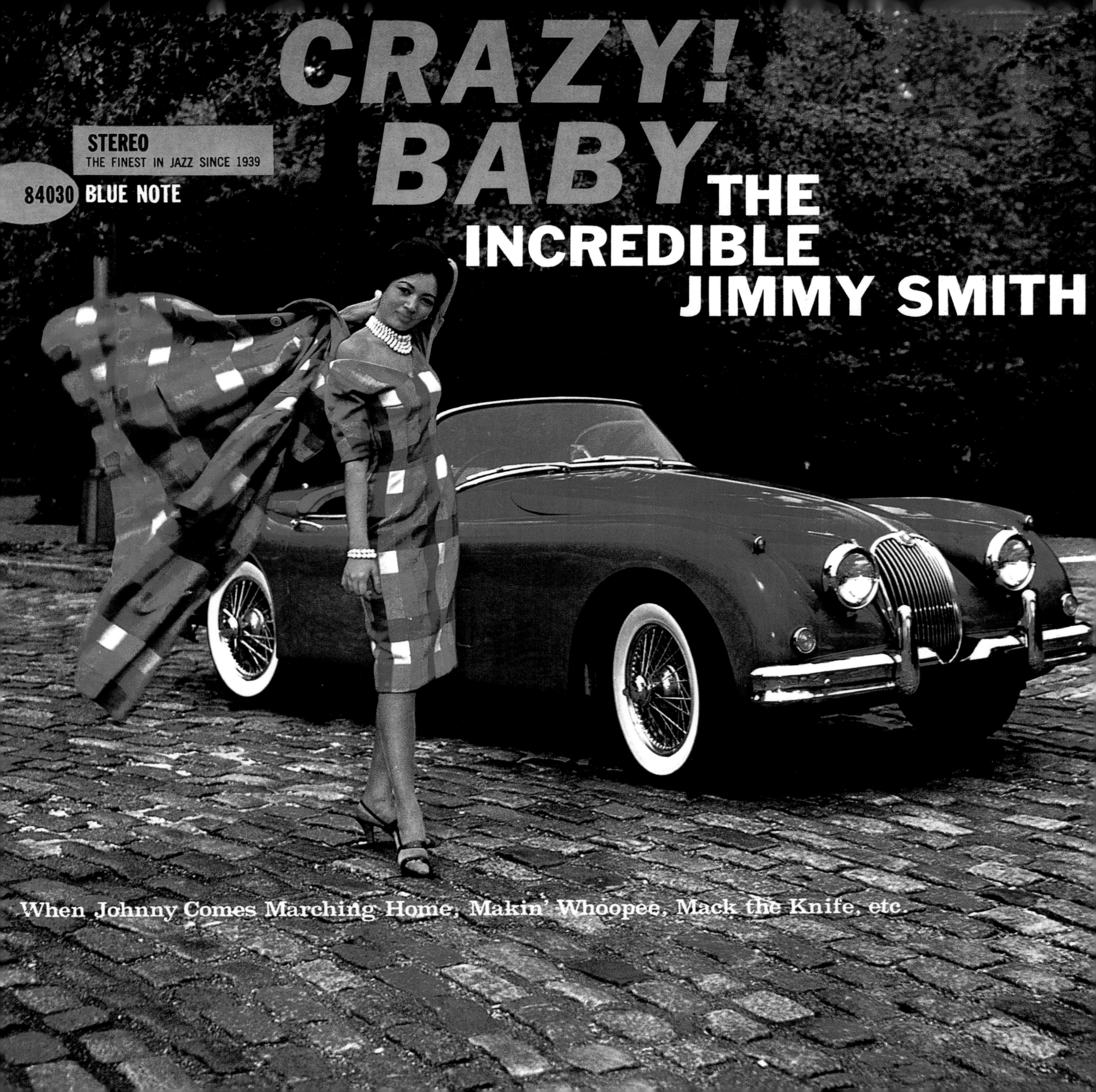

CRAZY!
BABY
STEREO
THE FINEST IN JAZZ SINCE 1939
84030 BLUE NOTE
THE
INCREDIBLE
JIMMY SMITH
When Johnny Comes Marching Home, Makin' Whoopee, Mack the Knife, etc.

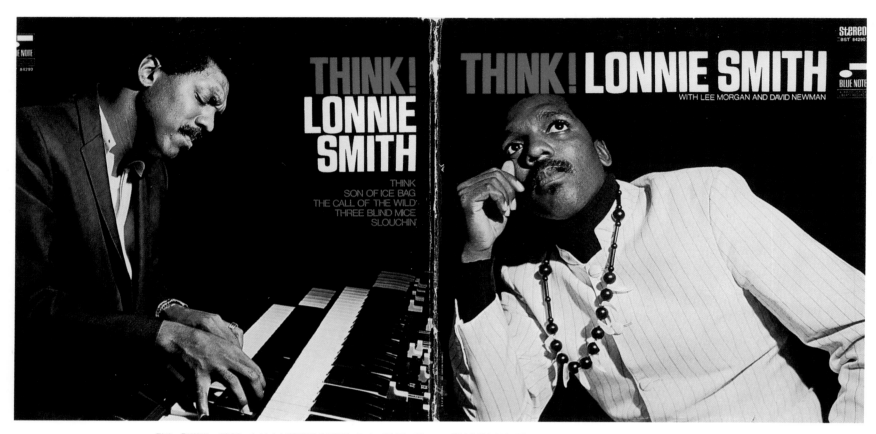

Title THINK 4290 Artist LONNIE SMITH Date 1968 Photos FRANCIS WOLFF Design FORLENZA VENOSA ASSOCIATES

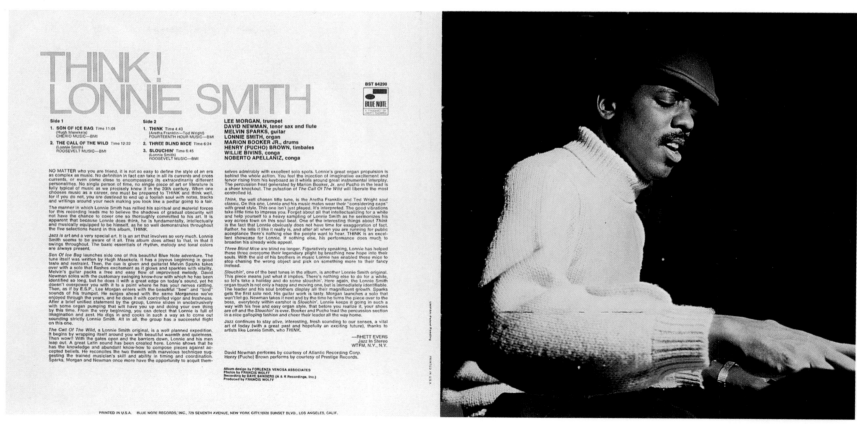

Liner Photo FRANCIS WOLFF

Opposite: Title DIMENSIONS & EXTENSIONS 4261 Artist SAM RIVERS Date 1967 Photo FRANCIS WOLFF Design REID MILES

STEREO
THE FINEST IN JAZZ SINCE 1939
84261 BLUE NOTE

DIMENSIONS & EXTENSIONS + SAM RIVERS

Title NEW YORK IS NOW 4287 Artist ORNETTE COLEMAN Date 1968 Photos FRANCIS WOLFF Design FORLENZA VENOSA ASSOCIATES

Liner Photos FRANCIS WOLFF

Opposite: Title SYMPHONY FOR IMPROVISERS 4247 Artist BON CHERRY Date 1966 Photo FRANCIS WOLFF Design REID MILES

SYMPHONY
FOR
IMPROVISERS
DON
CHERRY

BLP 4247

THE FINEST IN JAZZ SINCE 1939
BLUE NOTE
A PRODUCT OF LIBERTY RECORDS

PRINTED IN U.S.A.

© LIBERTY RECORDS, INC

Title AT THE HALF NOTE CAFE Vol. 1 4060
Artist DONALD BYRD
Date 1960
Design REID MILES

"Alfred said that he was never happier than
when in the midst of a recording session that was
going well. These recording sessions were
the very life's blood of the Blue Note experience."
RUTH LION

Title AT THE HALF NOTE CAFE Vol. 2 4061
Artist DONALD BYRD
Date 1960
Design REID MILES

Opposite: Title HERE WE COME 4088 Artist THE THREE SOUNDS Date 1960 Photo RONNIE BRATHWAITE

Here We Come
The 3 Sounds

STEREO
THE FINEST IN JAZZ SINCE 1939

84088 BLUE NOTE

Gene Harris / Andrew Simpkins
Bill Dowdy

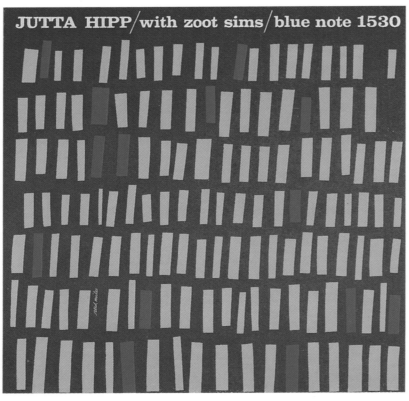

Title JUTTA HIPP WITH ZOOT SIMS 1530
Artist JUTTA HIPP
Date 1956
Design REID MILES

Title PAUL CHAMBERS QUINTET 1564
Artist PAUL CHAMBERS
Date 1957
Design TOM HANNAN

Title HANK MOBLEY QUINTET BNJ 61006
Artist HANK MOBLEY
Date RELEASED JAPAN ONLY 1984
Original Design TOM HANNAN

Title HANK 1560
Artist HANK MOBLEY
Date 1957
Design TOM HANNAN

Opposite: Title PATTERNS IN JAZZ 1517 Artist GIL MELLE Date 1956 Design REID MILES

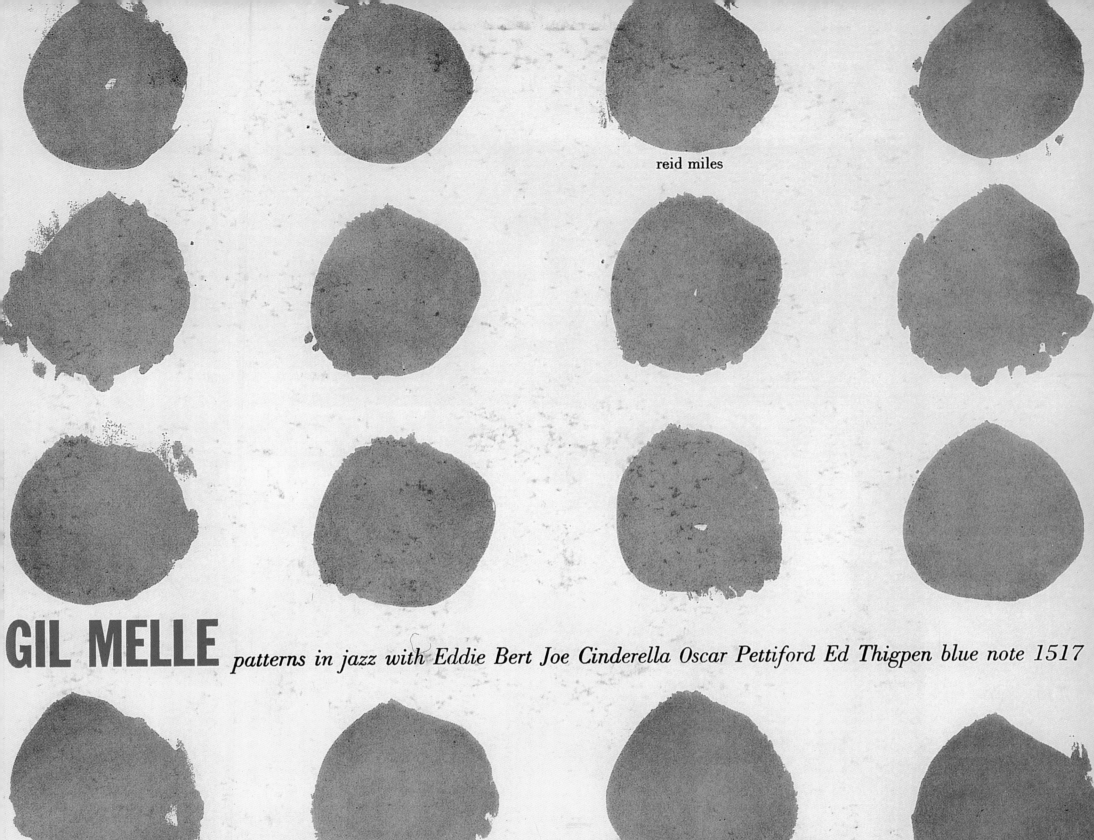

reid miles

GIL MELLE *patterns in jazz with Eddie Bert Joe Cinderella Oscar Pettiford Ed Thigpen blue note 1517*

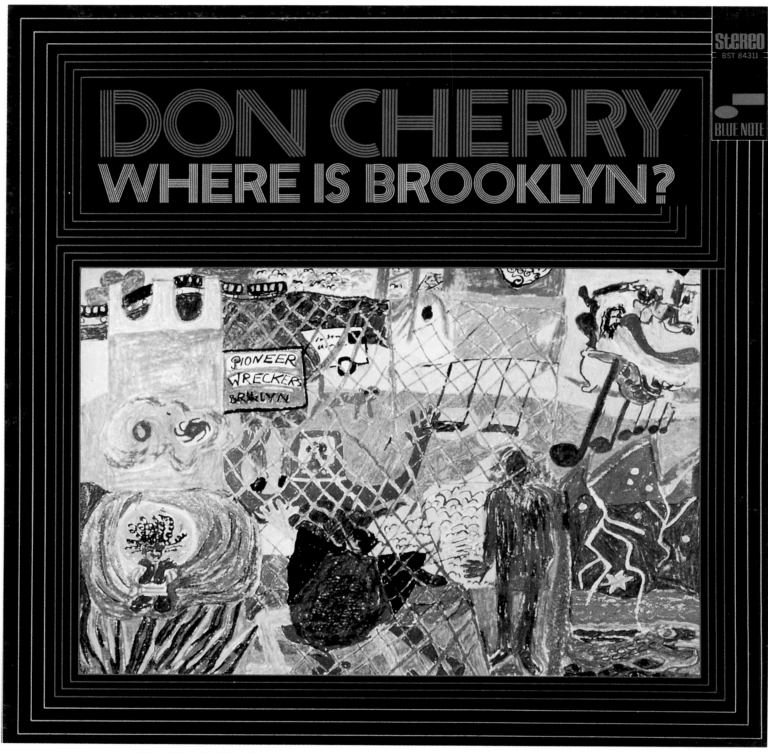

Title WHERE IS BROOKLYN? 4311 Artist DON CHERRY Date 1966 Painting MOQUI Design MATT DELFINO

Opposite: Title THE EMPTY FOXHOLE 4246 Artist ORNETTE COLEMAN Date 1966 Painting ORNETTE COLEMAN Design BOB FUENTES

THE FINEST IN JAZZ SINCE 1939
BLUE NOTE
A PRODUCT OF LIBERTY RECORDS

RNETTE COLEMAN / THE EMPTY FOXHOLE

Title BONE & BARI 1572
Artist CURTIS FULLER
Date 1957
Photo FRANCIS WOLFF
Design TOM HANNAN

Title A NEW SOUND – A NEW STAR 1512
Artist JIMMY SMITH
Date 1956
Photo FRANCIS WOLFF
Design REID MILES

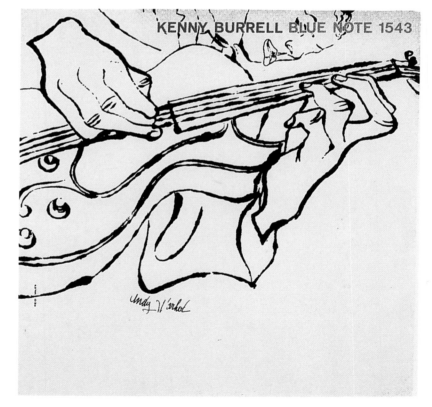

Title CANDY 1590
Artist LEE MORGAN
Date 1958
Photo EMERICK BRONSON
Design REID MILES

Title KENNY BURRELL Vol. 2 1543
Artist KENNY BURRELL
Date 1956
Illustration ANDY WARHOL
Design REID MILES

Opposite: Title IT JUST GOT TO BE 4120 Artist THE THREE SOUNDS Date 1960 Photo FRANCIS WOLFF Design REID MILES

STEREO
THE FINEST IN JAZZ SINCE 1939

84120 BLUE NOTE

THE THREE SOUNDS

IT JUST GOT TO BE

Title PUTTIN' IT TOGETHER 4282
Artist ELVIN JONES
Date 1968
Photo FRANCIS WOLFF
Design FORLENZA VENOSA ASSOCIATES

Title DETROIT – NEW YORK JUNCTION 1513
Artist THAD JONES
Date 1956
Photo FRANCIS WOLFF
Design REID MILES

Title HERBIE NICHOLS TRIO 1519
Artist HERBIE NICHOLS
Date 1956
Photo FRANCIS WOLFF
Design REID MILES

Title FEELIN' GOOD 4072
Artist THE THREE SOUNDS
Date 1960
Photo FRANCIS WOLFF
Design REID MILES

Opposite: Title AFRICAN HIGH LIFE 4136 Artist SOLOMON ILORI Date 1963 Photo and Design REID MILES

SOLOMON
ILORI
AND HIS AFRO-DRUM ENSEMBLE
AFRICAN
HIGH
LIFE

THE FINEST IN JAZZ SINCE 1939

4136 BLUE NOTE

Title LEE MORGAN 4901 Artist LEE MORGAN Date 1972 Photo NORMAN SEEFF Design JOAN MARKER Hand Lettering TIM CLARK

Title SCHIZOPHRENIA 4297
Artist WAYNE SHORTER
Date 1967
Photo JOHN ZOINER

Title THE SIXTH SENSE 4335
Artist LEE MORGAN
Date 1967
Photo FRANCIS WOLFF
Design BOB VENOSA/HAVONA

Opposite: Title GENESIS 4369 Artist ELVIN JONES Date 1971 Photo NORMAN SEEFF Design JOHN CABALKA
Overleaf: Title CHARISMA 4312 Artist LEE MORGAN Date 1966 Design ANN MEISEL

Genesis *Elvin Jones*

BLUE NOTE

LEE MORGAN CHARISMA

HEY CHICO
SOMETHIN' CUTE
RAINY NIGHT
SWEET HONEY BEE
THE MURPHY MAN
THE DOUBLE UP

BLUE NOTE RECORDS, INC. • A DIVISION OF LIBERTY RECORDS • NEW YORK, NEW YORK 10019

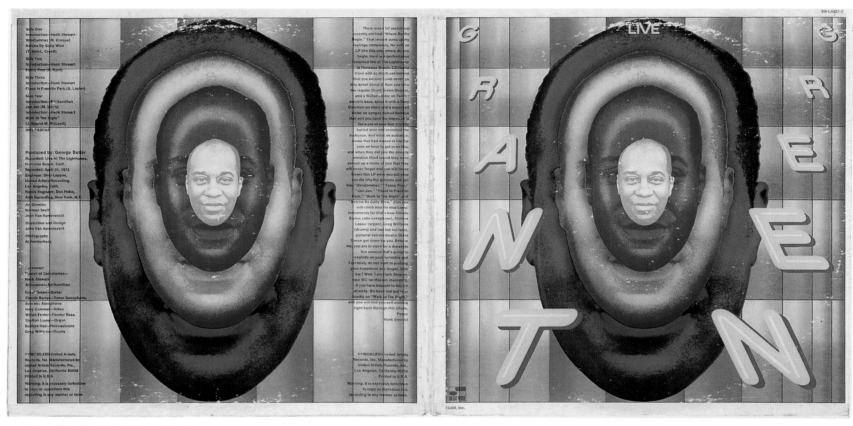

Title LIVE AT THE LIGHTHOUSE BN-LA037-62 Artist GRANT GREEN Date 1972 Cover and Liner Photo AL VANDENBERG Illustration and Design JOHN VAN HAMERSVELD

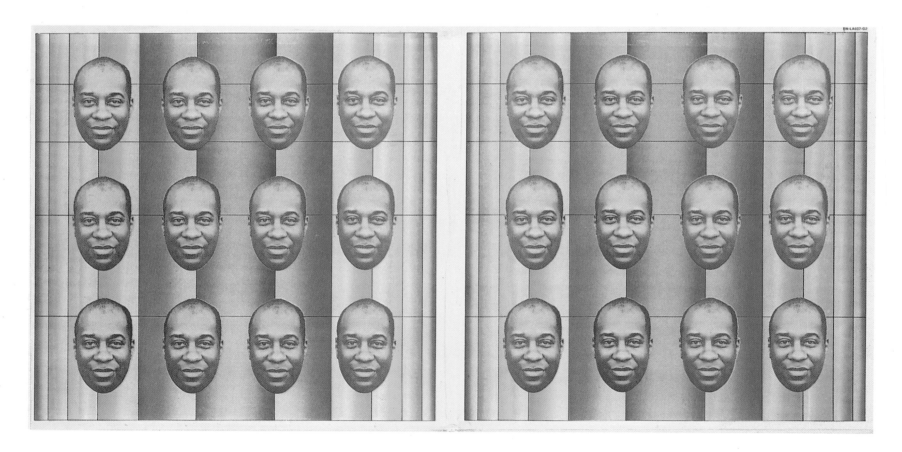

Opposite: Title MR. JONES BN-LA110-F Artist ELVIN JONES Date 1972 Painting PHILIP HAYES Design LLOYD ZIFF

Mr. Jones

Elvin Jones

Blue Note

PHILIP HAYS

COVER STORY 2

In 1965 Alfred Lion and Francis Wolff sold Blue Note to Liberty. The label had dominated the artistic and commercial courses of jazz for a decade, but the stress of operating an independent record label for 26 years had taken its toll. They needed the financial clout of a pop label to ease the strain of daily business, which Liberty's offer provided.

Late 1966 saw Horace Silver record *The Jody Grind*, Blue Note's first album issued with a gatefold sleeve. Liner notes and musician mug shots were now displayed inside, which allowed the cover to open into a double image of Silver in suede flanked by girls à la mode. Reid Miles' design and colour photography captured perfectly the swinging 60s ethos.

It was not surprising that such a free spirit as Alfred Lion never fully adjusted to the demands of corporate structure. In 1967 this dissatisfaction, compounded by health problems, led to his retirement from the company. The same year Reid Miles ended his 11-year run as label designer to begin a full-time career in photography.

With their departure at the psychedelic end of the 60s, changes were inevitable. In 1969, Liberty was bought by the United Artists group. Francis Wolff remained at Blue Note, producing some fine straight ahead sessions. But with his death in 1971 and the new directions in music, the label's emphasis shifted with commercial success towards funk and fusion.

The innovation and continuity of design that Reid Miles brought to Blue Note during the previous two decades is lacking from the label's 70s output, but sleeves such as Grant Green's *Live At The Lighthouse* and Elvin Jones' *Genesis* still managed to capture the essence of their time.

GLYN CALLINGHAM

Title BLUE MODE 4343
Artist REUBEN WILSON
Date 1969
Photo BOB VENOSA
Cover Art MATI KLARWEIN

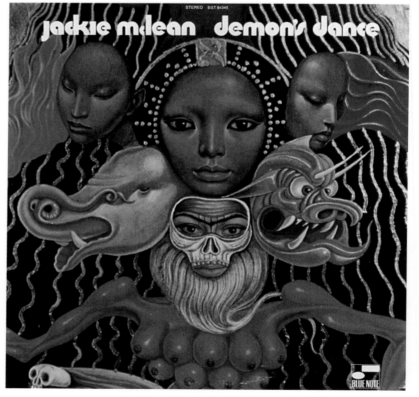

Title DEMON'S DANCE 4345
Artist JACKIE MCLEAN
Date 1967
Design BOB VENOSA

Opposite: Title OF LOVE AND PEACE 4242 Artist LARRY YOUNG Date 1966 Photo and Design REID MILES
Overleaf: Title MIDNIGHT CREEPER 4280 Artist LOU DONALDSON Date 1968 Photo JOEL BRODSKY Design FORLENZA VENOSA ASSOCIATES

BLP 4242

BLUE NOTE

LARRY YOUNG
OF LOVE AND PEACE

BLUE NOTE
A PRODUCT OF
LIBERTY RECORDS

BST 84280

LOU DONALDSON
MIDNIGHT CREEPER

Featuring
LOU DONALDSON
BLUE MITCHELL
GEORGE BENSON
LONNIE SMITH
LEO MORRIS

BLUE NOTE
A PRODUCT OF
LIBERTY RECORDS

LOU DONALDSON
MIDNIGHT CREEPER

MIDNIGHT CREEPER LOVE POWER DAPPER DAN ELIZABETH BAG OF JEWELS

Title VIBRATIONS 4248
Artist THE THREE SOUNDS
Date 1965
Photo and Design REID MILES

Title OUT OF THIS WORLD 4197
Artist THE THREE SOUNDS
Date 1962
Photo and Design REID MILES

Title MY HOUR OF NEED 9001
Artist DODO GREENE
Date 1962
Photo FRANCIS WOLFF
Design LARRY MILLER

Title LUSH LIFE 4254
Artist LOU DONALDSON
Date 1967
Photo FRANCIS WOLFF
Design REID MILES

Opposite: Title MOODS 4044 Artist THE THREE SOUNDS Date 1960 Photo HUGH BELL Model RUTH MASON

Moods

the
3 sounds

"In the 50s, Rudy Van Gelder was just
getting started when his friend Gil Melle took Alfred
over to his studio in Hackensack, New
Jersey. The rest is recording history. Rudy developed
the distinctive 'Blue Note Sound' and, at
the same time, became one of the most sought after
sound engineers in jazz."
RUTH LION

Title AT THE HICKORY HOUSE Vol. 1 1515
Artist JUTTA HIPP
Date 1956
Photo FRANCIS WOLFF
Design REID MILES

Title AT THE HICKORY HOUSE Vol. 2 1516
Artist JUTTA HIPP
Date 1956
Photo FRANCIS WOLFF
Design REID MILES

Opposite: Title PORTRAIT OF SHEILA 9002 Artist SHEILA JORDAN Date 1962 Photo ZIGGY WILLMANN Design REID MILES

PORTRAIT OF SHEILA

SHEILA JORDAN

BARRY GALBRAITH / GUITAR **STEVE SWALLOW** / BASS **DENZIL BEST** / DRUMS

STEREO
THE FINEST IN JAZZ SINCE 1939

89002 BLUE NOTE

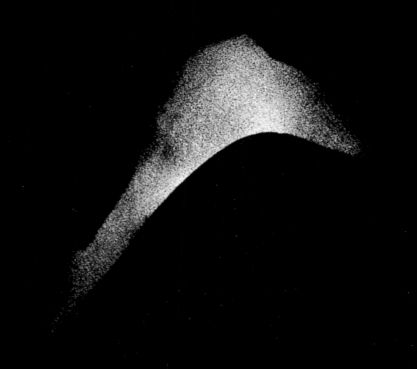

Title THE JODY GRIND 4250 Artist HORACE SILVER Date 1966 Cover Photos and Design REID MILES

Liner Photos FRANCIS WOLFF

Opposite: Title MR. SHING-A-LING 4271 Artist LOU DONALDSON Date 1967 Photo and Design REID MILES

Ode To Billie Joe / The Shadow Of Your Smile / The Humpback / Peepin' / The Kid

LOU DONALDSON

MR. SHING-A-LING

THE FINEST IN JAZZ SINCE 1939

BLUE NOTE

A PRODUCT OF LIBERTY RECORDS

Title LOVE CALL 4356
Artist ORNETTE COLEMAN
Date 1968
Photo FRANCIS WOLFF
Design HAVONA

Title SERENADE TO A SOUL SISTER 4277
Artist HORACE SILVER
Date 1968
Photo BILLY COBHAM
Design FORLENZA VENOSA ASSOCIATES

Title 'BOUT SOUL 4284
Artist JACKIE MCLEAN
Date 1967
Photo CHARLES KEDDIE
Design FORLENZA VENOSA ASSOCIATES

Title THAT CERTAIN FEELING 4281
Artist JOHN PATTON
Date 1968
Photo JOEL BRODSKY
Design FORLENZA VENOSA ASSOCIATES

Opposite: Title THE PHANTOM 4293 Artist DUKE PEARSON Date 1968 Photo FRANCIS WOLFF Design FORLENZA VENOSA ASSOCIATES

STEREO
BST 84293

duke pearson
the phantom
featuring bobby hutcherson

BLUE NOTE

Title SLOW DRAG 4292 Artist DONALD BYRD Date 1967 Cover Photos CHARLES KEDDIE Design FORLENZA VENOSA ASSOCIATES

Liner Photos FRANCIS WOLFF

Opposite: Title THE FLIP 4329 Artist HANK MOBLEY Date 1969 Design BOB VENOSA/HAVONA
Overleaf: Title CARAMBA! 4289 Artist LEE MORGAN Date 1968 Photo CHARLES KEDDIE Design FORLENZA VENOSA ASSOCIATES

STEREO BST-84329

HANK
MOBLEY
THE
FLIP

BLUE NOTE

lee morgan
¡caramba!

CARAMBA
SUICIDE CITY
CUNNING LEE
SOULITA
HELEN'S RITUAL

BLUE NOTE
A PRODUCT OF
LIBERTY RECORDS

BST 84289

lee morgan
¡caramba!

LEE MORGAN BENNIE MAUPIN CEDAR WALTON REGINALD WORKMAN BILLY HIGGINS

STEREO
BST 84289

BLUE NOTE

COVER STORY 3

Alfred Lion's Blue Note had always put quality above cost. If he felt a session had been unsuccessful, it was shelved. His high standards are best illustrated by a handwritten report he made for an unissued date: 'This session would be okay for release, but it is just not up to Blue Note's standards'. As a result stacks of tracks lay dormant in the label's vault.

In 1975 Michael Cuscuna and label executive Charlie Lourie began a programme to release this unheard material. It was to run until 1981, making great music available for the first time. Lee Morgan's *Tom Cat* and Hank Mobley's *A Slice of the Top* are prime examples from this series that did much to keep the old Blue Note sound alive. Unfortunately the sleeves they came in did not always fulfil a similar role for the classic Blue Note look.

The release of these sessions in Japan, where the label is revered, was a different cover story. New artwork was created in keeping with the Reid Miles tradition (see the selection on pages 100-107). Pressed in small quantities for the Japanese market these LPs, with their unique covers, have become collectors' items.

United Artists was absorbed in turn by EMI, and the revitalization of Blue Note began in 1984 when Bruce Lundvall at Capitol Records relaunched the label. A rich back catalogue, more unissued gems given cover designs to compliment the music's quality and period (see this page and opposite), combined with new recording plans secured Blue Note's future.

GLYN CALLINGHAM

Title FAR AWAY LANDS 4425
Artist HANK MOBLEY
Date RELEASED 1984
Photo DON HUNSTEIN
Design RICHARD MANTEL/MANTEL KOPPEL & SCHER

Title BORN TO BE BLUE 4432
Artist GRANT GREEN
Date RELEASED 1985
Photo CHARLES STEWART
Design TERRY KOPPEL/KOPPEL & SCHER

Opposite: Title STRAIGHT NO FILTER 4435 Artist HANK MOBLEY Date RELEASED 1986 Photo FRANCIS WOLFF

HANK
MOBLEY

STRAIGHT NO FILTER

THE FINEST IN JAZZ SINCE 1939

BLUE NOTE

Title NIGERIA GXK 8180
Artist GRANT GREEN
Date RELEASED JAPAN ONLY 1981
Illustration T. FUJIYAMA

Title GOODEN'S CORNER GXF 3058
Artist GRANT GREEN
Date RELEASED JAPAN ONLY 1979
Illustration T. FUJIYAMA

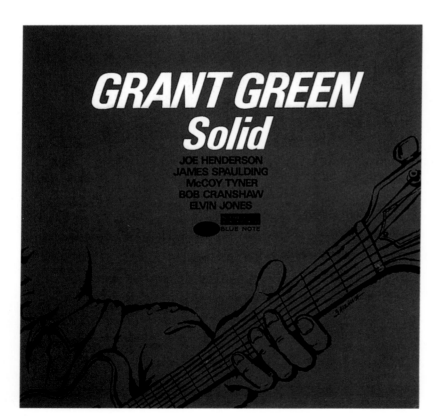

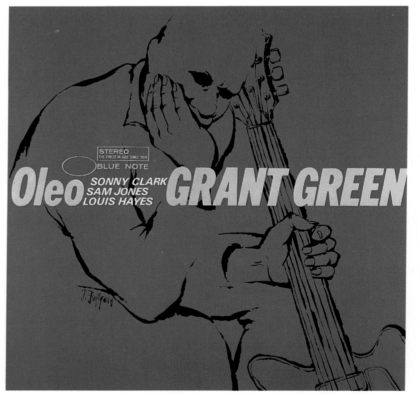

Title SOLID GXK 8187
Artist GRANT GREEN
Date RELEASED JAPAN ONLY 1981
Design GORO KUNISADA
Illustration SHINJI AIZAWA

Title OLEO GXF 3065
Artist GRANT GREEN
Date RELEASED JAPAN ONLY 1980
Illustration T. FUJIYAMA

Opposite: Title MATADOR GXF 3053 Artist GRANT GREEN Date RELEASED JAPAN ONLY 1979 Design T. TANAKA Illustration T. FUJIYAMA

MATADOR
STEREO
THE FINEST IN JAZZ SINCE 1939
BLUE NOTE
GRANT GREEN
McCOY TYNER
BOB CRANSHAW
ELVIN JONES

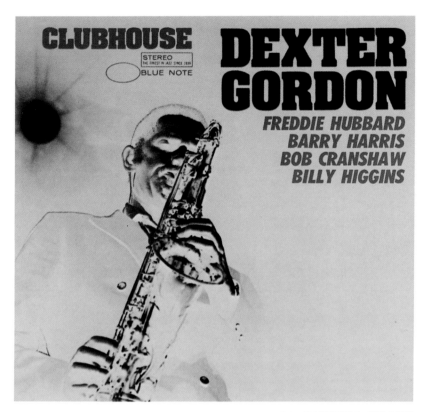

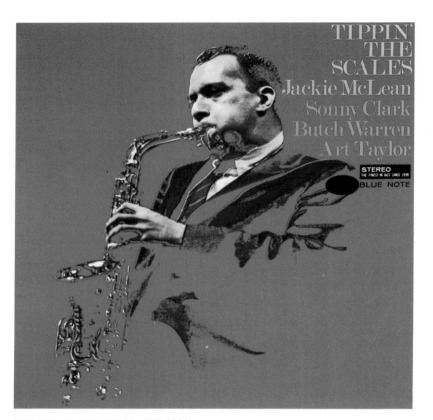

Title CLUBHOUSE GXF 3055
Artist DEXTER GORDON
Date RELEASED JAPAN ONLY 1979
Photo AKIYOSHI MIYASHITA
Design TOSHIKAZU TANAKA

Title TIPPIN' THE SCALES GXF 3062
Artist JACKIE MCLEAN
Date RELEASED JAPAN ONLY 1979
Photo and Design K. ABE

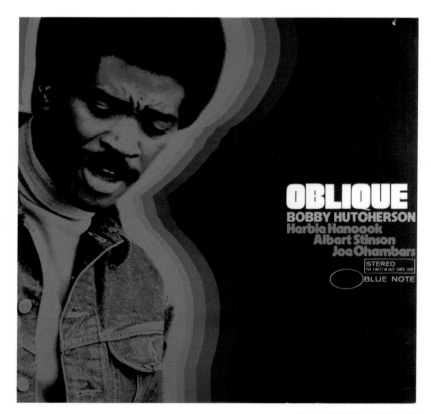

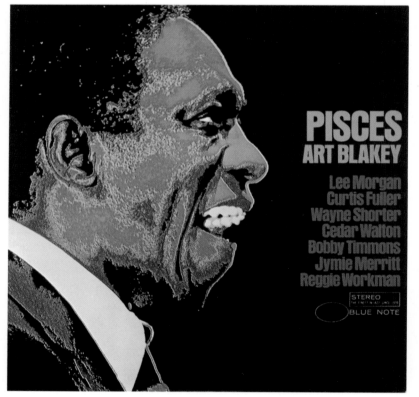

Title OBLIQUE GXF 3061
Artist BOBBY HUTCHERSON
Date RELEASED JAPAN ONLY 1979
Photo and Design K. ABE

Title PISCES GXK 8151
Artist ART BLAKEY
Date RELEASED JAPAN ONLY 1980
Photo and Design K. ABE

Title POPPIN' GXF 3066
Artist Hank Mobley
Date RELEASED JAPAN ONLY 1980
Photo K. ABE

Title THINKING OF HOME GXK 8188
Artist HANK MOBLEY
Date RELEASED JAPAN ONLY 1981
Design SHINJI AIZAWA

Title CONSEQUENCE GXK 8172
Artist JACKIE MCLEAN
Date RELEASED JAPAN ONLY 1981

Title CHANT GXK 8183
Artist DONALD BYRD
Date RELEASED JAPAN ONLY 1981
Design SHINJI AIZAWA

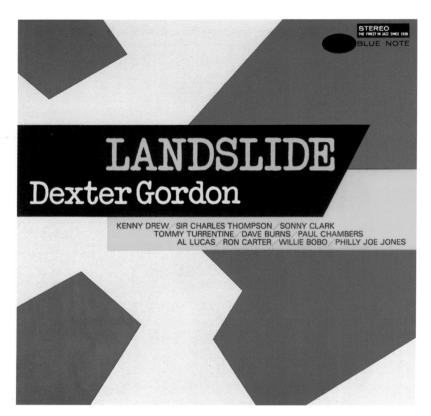

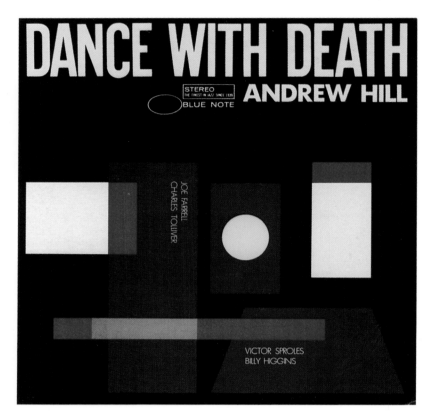

Title LANDSLIDE GXK 8175
Artist DEXTER GORDON
Date RELEASED JAPAN ONLY 1981

Title DANCE WITH DEATH GXK 8184
Artist ANDREW HILL
Date RELEASED JAPAN ONLY 1981
Design SHINJI AIZAWA

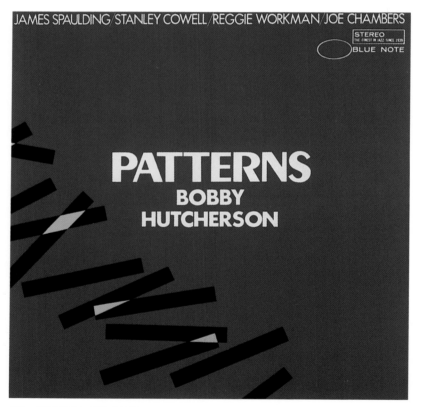

Title THE JACKIE MCLEAN QUINTET LNJ 80118
Artist JACKIE MCLEAN
Date RELEASED JAPAN ONLY 1978

Title PATTERNS GXK 8185
Artist BOBBY HUTCHERSON
Date RELEASED JAPAN ONLY 1981
Design SHINJI AIZAWA

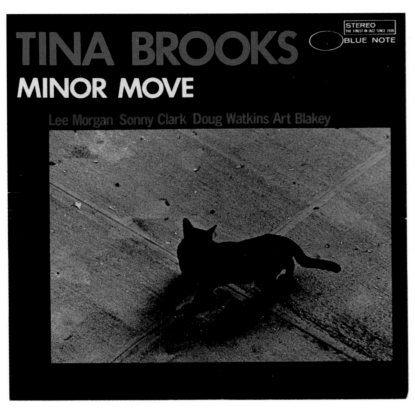

Title MINOR MOVE GXF 3072
Artist TINA BROOKS
Date RELEASED JAPAN ONLY 1980
Photo TADAYUKI NAITOH

Title A SLICE OF THE TOP GXK 8177
Artist HANK MOBLEY
Date RELEASED JAPAN ONLY 1981

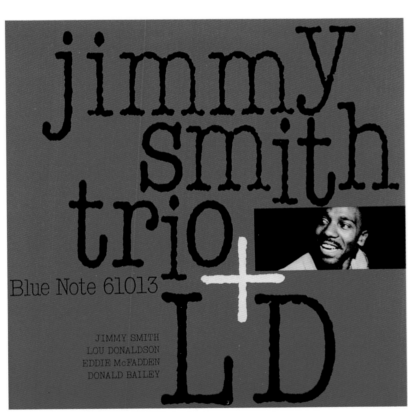

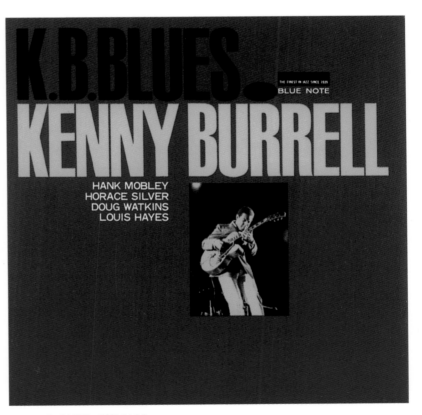

Title JIMMY SMITH TRIO + LD BNJ 61013
Artist JIMMY SMITH
Date RELEASED JAPAN ONLY 1985
Photo FRANCIS WOLFF

Title K.B. BLUES GXK 8154
Artist KENNY BURRELL
Date RELEASED JAPAN ONLY 1980
Design TOSHIKAZU TANAKA

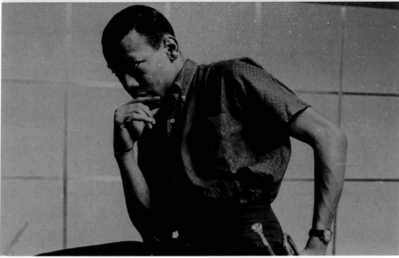

Title SEXTET GXF 3024
Artist LEE MORGAN
Date RELEASED JAPAN ONLY 1978
Photo CHARLES STEWART
Design FUJIYAMA

Title ALL-STAR SEXTET GXF 3023
Artist LEE MORGAN
Date RELEASED JAPAN ONLY 1978
Photo CHARLES STEWART
Design FUJIYAMA

Title SONIC BOOM GXK 8171
Artist LEE MORGAN
Date RELEASED JAPAN ONLY 1981

Title TOMCAT GXK 8181
Artist LEE MORGAN
Date RELEASED JAPAN ONLY 1981
Art Direction GORO KUNISADA

Opposite: Title SPIRAL GXK 8178 Artist BOBBY HUTCHERSON Date RELEASED JAPAN ONLY 1981 Photo KATSUJI ABE

COVER STORY 4

The compact disc with extended playing time and user friendly nature will be the format that replays Blue Note into the next century.

If there is a future for the label on vinyl, it will be in a selective way. Shown on pages 110-111 are covers from the Connoisseur series, limited edition reissues of rare albums. While on this page and opposite, are examples of Capitol's 1995 Rare Groove series, previously unissued funk from the vaults. All these covers feature Francis Wolff's evocative colour photography combined with contempory designs by Patrick Roques.

The era of the LP is now over, consigned to audio history. Compact discs confined by their postage stamp graphics seem unlikely to surpass the innovative opportunities offered by the 12-inch canvas on which Reid Miles created so many design classics.

In their heyday Blue Note's fine-cuts and bespoke covers were the coolest combination around.

GLYN CALLINGHAM

Title KOFI BI-31875
Artist DONALD BYRD
Date RELEASED 1995
Photo FRANCIS WOLFF
Design PATRICK ROQUES

Title THE SCORPION BI-31876
Artist LOU DONALDSON
Date RELEASED 1995
Photo FRANCIS WOLFF
Design PATRICK ROQUES

Opposite: Title BOOGALOO BI-31878 Artist JOHN PATTON Date RELEASED 1995 Photo FRANCIS WOLFF Design PATRICK ROQUES

STEREO   31878

john
patton
boogaloo

BLUE NOTE

STEREO
HANK MOBLEY A SLICE OF THE TOP

STEREO
33582 BLUE NOTE

Hank Mobley / James Spaulding / Lee Morgan / Kiane Zawadi / Howard Johnson / McCoy Tyner / Bob Cranshaw / Billy Higgins

Title A SLICE OF THE TOP BI-33582
Artist HANK MOBLEY
Date RELEASED 1995
Photo FRANCIS WOLFF
Design PATRICK ROQUES

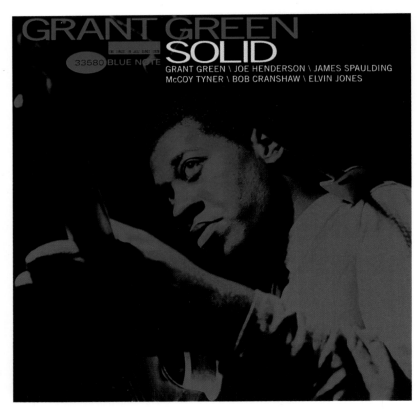

GRANT GREEN
SOLID
GRANT GREEN \ JOE HENDERSON \ JAMES SPAULDING
McCOY TYNER \ BOB CRANSHAW \ ELVIN JONES

33580 BLUE NOTE

Title SOLID BI-33580
Artist GRANT GREEN
Date RELEASED 1995
Photo FRANCIS WOLFF
Design PATRICK ROQUES

LEE MORGAN
LEE MORGAN/WAYNE SHORTER/BOBBY HUTCHERSON/HERBIE HANCOCK/
RON CARTER/BILLY HIGGINS

THE PROCRASTINATOR

STEREO
33579 BLUE NOTE

Title THE PROCRASTINATOR BI-33579
Artist LEE MORGAN
Date RELEASED 1995
Photo FRANCIS WOLFF
Design PATRICK ROQUES

STEREO
ETC
etcetera
WAYNE SHORTER/HERBIE HANCOCK/CECIL MCBEE/JOE CHAMBERS
WAYNE SHORTER

33581 BLUE NOTE

Title ETCETERA BI-33581
Artist WAYNE SHORTER
Date RELEASED 1995
Photo FRANCIS WOLFF
Design PATRICK ROQUES

Opposite: Title PATTERNS BI-33583 Artist BOBBY HUTCHERSON Date RELEASED 1995 Photo FRANCIS WOLFF Design PATRICK ROQUES

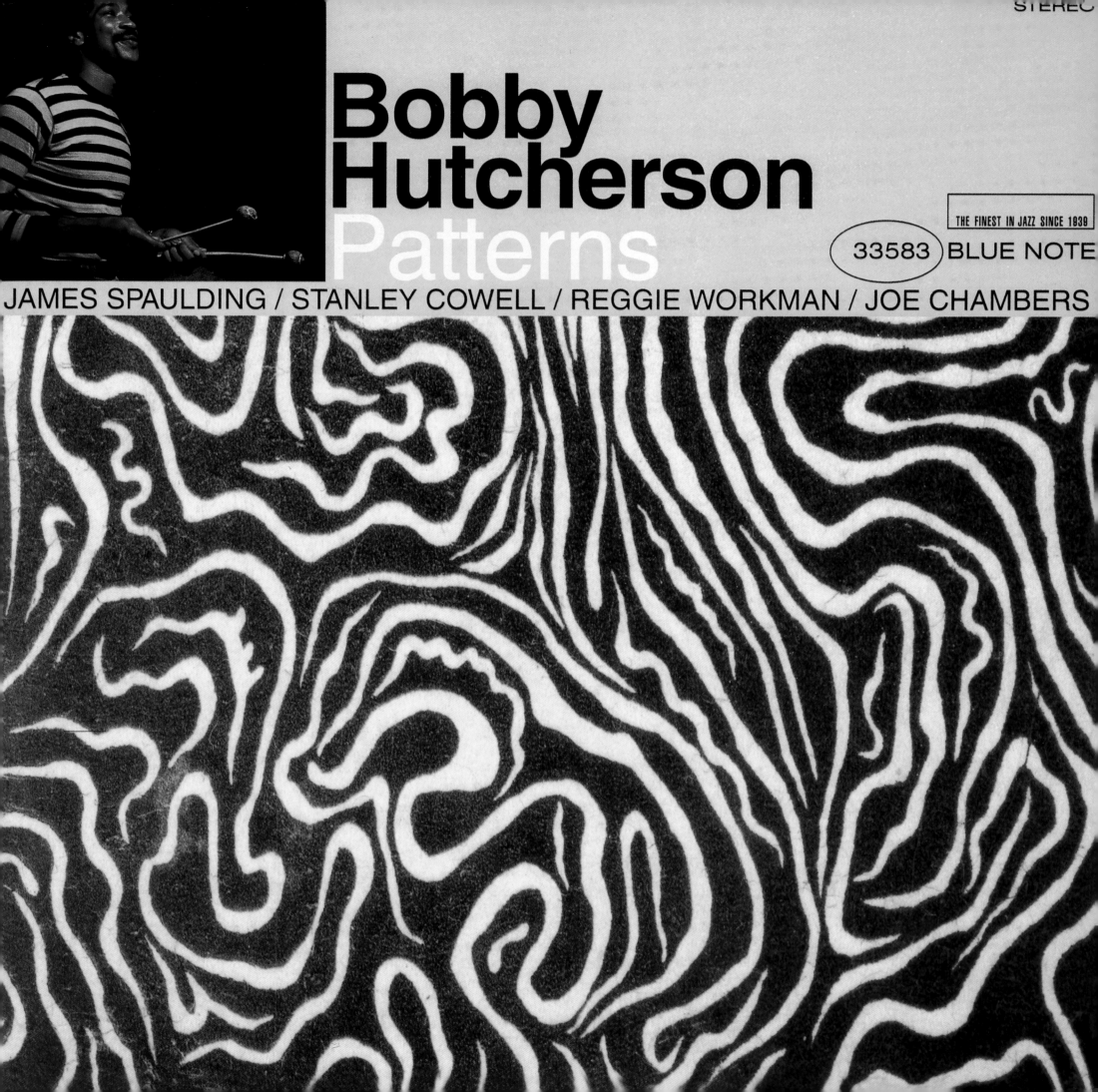

PREVIOUSLY RELEASED

The Cover Art of Blue Note
Graham Marsh, Glyn Callingham
and Felix Cromey

The jazz record company Blue Note has always
had a reputation for producing fine album
covers and this is a comprehensive,
album sized collection of the very best.

"...revives a peerless legacy."
Vogue Magazine

California Cool
Graham Marsh and Glyn Callingham

The album covers of this book reflect the new,
laid-back West Coast sound of the American
jazz scene of the 1950s.

"Buy the book, then play the music."
GQ Magazine

East Coasting
Graham Marsh and Glyn Callingham

East Coasting returns to the American east
coast of the 1950s and 1960s to draw on the
records that were released on the Prestige,
Atlantic and Riverside labels.

"...splendid and rather beautiful."
Q Magazine

ALSO AVAILABLE
The Blues Album Cover Art – Graham Marsh and Barrie Lewis